Adventures in Teaching
MILITARY BRATS

Adventures in Teaching
MILITARY BRATS
Travels, Recipes, and Tips

ROSE PORTER

Archway Publishing books may be ordered through booksellers or by contacting:

Archway Publishing
1663 Liberty Drive
Bloomington, IN 47403
www.archwaypublishing.com
1 (888) 242-5904

Because of the dynamic nature of the Internet, any web addresses or links contained in this book may have changed since publication and may no longer be valid. The views expressed in this work are solely those of the author and do not necessarily reflect the views of the publisher, and the publisher hereby disclaims any responsibility for them.

Any people depicted in stock imagery provided by Thinkstock are models, and such images are being used for illustrative purposes only.
Certain stock imagery © Thinkstock.

ISBN: 978-1-4808-1922-1 (sc)
ISBN: 978-1-4808-1923-8 (e)

Library of Congress Control Number: 2015909887

Print information available on the last page.

Archway Publishing rev. date: 07/28/2015

Dedication

FOR MANY YEARS TEACHERS HAVE BEEN ENCOURAGING ME TO WRITE A BOOK. I always thought they were nuts! I'd never written anything for public consideration, but this year, after my retirement from the Department of Defense Dependent Schools (DoDDS), I decided to give it a try. I'd been teaching for DoDDS for thirty-four years and had plenty of stories to tell.

This book is a combination of memories of the countries where I've taught the military children, my travels during that time, and the recipes I've gathered and added to my own collection.

This book is dedicated to DoDDS teachers, past and present, for all they represent to our military. Our military's children have been blessed to have us, and we have been blessed to teach them all over the world.

CHAPTER 1

In the Beginning

ALL OF US HAVE TAUGHT SOMEONE SOMEWHERE SOMETHING; NOT MANY HAVE MADE it their life's work. I always loved my teachers and loved the school experience, until I hit high school. High school was not as much fun, but it was necessary if you wanted to get into college. I went to college because that was the only way I could become a professional teacher and work with children.

My first two years at Miami-Dade Junior College in Miami, Florida, were great. Religion, philosophy, psychology, music, and the arts were just some of the reasons why. It was all new information. Then came the School of Education, and I went back to my old way of thinking: education was a necessary means to becoming a teacher, at least in the legal sense.

The greatest thing about life at the University of South Florida in Tampa was hearing about the Department of Defense Dependent Schools (DoDDS) for the first time. It made all the years of boring homework, projects, and lectures worth the time, effort, and expense!

The DoDDS are located on or near US military's installations all around the world. The word around campus was that you needed two years teaching experience and a master's degree before bothering to apply. Only the very best applicants would be interviewed for possible placement.

I was excited; I knew I would get a job. I knew I would absolutely enjoy living and teaching in Europe. I just had to finish at University of South Florida, teach for two years, and finish a master's. No problem! I was young and single.

I graduated with a degree in elementary education, early childhood, and supervision, and I got a job teaching kindergarten in Miami. My therapy during the first semester of kindergarten was to learn to knit and to complete an afghan. The second semester, I started a master's program at Florida Atlantic University in Boca Raton. My partner in the kindergarten building had been teaching for ten years, but when I started working on my master's, she decided she had to start too. We drove for an hour after school to Boca and took classes for twelve long months. I had a deadline to meet, so the second year I started taking two classes a week.

I had applied with DoDDS around February and had an interview scheduled in April. I took a day off school and flew to Orlando. I was officially hired two weeks later.

They told me in my interview that all the openings were in the Philippines, which was fine with me. They offered me a kindergarten/art slot in Argentia, Newfoundland, at the K-12 navy school.

I had never seen snow. The Philippines would have been perfect! I was shocked but very excited by the idea of Canada. So what if I had no winter clothes, no snow boots, no hats, gloves, or coats? I was leaving Florida. For a native Floridian, leaving was harder than I thought it would be. I used to leave my Miami school in the afternoons, race home to change clothes, and hit the beach for one to two hours of sun. I always had a tan, but then, everybody who lives in Florida has a tan. No big deal.

✤ CHAPTER 2 ✤

1972–1973
Argentia, Newfoundland

MY EDITOR ADVISED ME TO REWRITE THIS CHAPTER AND MAKE IT MORE POSITIVE. So I took my laptop and a copy of the book with me to Pisa for a week of Italian cooking classes. I thought the Italian atmosphere would help my creativity. It didn't work. I reread the chapter several times and decided I had to leave it the way it was. Newfoundland was not a great year for me for several reasons. If I'd been raised in Minnesota or New York, Newfoundland would have seemed normal to me. Since I was a native Floridian, Newfoundland wasn't anywhere near normal. The experiences I had during my nine months weren't glamorous, but they kept me busy. I wanted to go to Europe, and I knew that the nine months in snowy, cold Newfoundland would enable me to do that. After all, I had volunteered to go anywhere, teach anything, if only I were hired by Uncle Sam. So I left chapter 2 alone. I hope my readers don't quit reading because it isn't positive enough. The other countries where I later taught and lived were better suited to my personality and more conducive to positive memories.

Arriving in Argentia in early August was exciting. I had gone to Bermuda to attend a workshop en route to the navy base. That was fun, but the fun turned to work once I got to school. No one goes to Bermuda for a week to learn new information only to keep it to oneself. One had to give workshops to the staff to pay back Uncle Sam. Nothing Uncle Sam gives its teachers is given freely.

Once the newness of teaching in Canada wore off, winter was officially in session. We had lots of sunny days, but temperatures were extremely frigid. The wind was always blowing—and not the warm breezes of Miami Beach, but the cold, wicked wind of the north! Men always wore hats, and the women wore scarves tightly tied to keep hairdos from being totally blown away.

Single teachers lived in the tallest building in Newfoundland, the navy's answer to one-stop living in deplorable conditions. The ten-story building housed the enlisted personnel, the married but unaccompanied, the unattached officers, the civilians (including teachers), the mess hall, the BOQ (bachelor officers quarters) facilities, library, and I don't remember what else! The mess hall served breakfast for ten cents. When you signed in each morning and paid your ten cents, you could also pick up a mimeographed copy of the latest news from the States and around the world. You read the copy and then shared it with another person at the breakfast table. There was no *Stars and Stripes* newspaper.

Going to see a navy doctor was a trip. Back in those days, our benefits included health insurance which we used with the military. It was deducted from our paychecks, just as it is done today. However, when we went to the dispensary, we still paid a flat fee—one dollar to see a doctor. Sometimes the corpsman would forget to collect our dollar, but never fear. Every now and then, the military would do a friendly audit and collect what we owed. Now it's funny, but then it was a sin to forget to pay your dollar for the doctor's services. It didn't matter who the doctor was—surgeon, general practitioner, or dentist.

The only reason I survived my assignment in Newfoundland was my principal. Whenever I looked depressed—which was quite often—he'd call me into his office, close the door, and tell me I was getting a transfer to Germany, but I had to stick it out until June. I had previously filled out a job application for a school district on the beach in sunny, warm California, but I tore it up. I really believed him. Now, looking back, I know he was just blowing smoke to keep me there. After all, the North Central Accreditation, NCA, was coming. I was the kindergarten and the art teacher, not only for the elementary kids but for the high school students as well.

I was not certified to teach art and had never considered taking the classes required for certification. My only talent was drawing stick figures and dull, boring rectangular houses, but somehow I was the art teacher. The elementary kids were easy; my strength was working with young children. One of the other teachers had torn every art project known to man out of her ten-year stack of *Instructor* magazines, and she lent me her file. Those projects were just right for the younger students.

High school was another story. We did pottery, batik, still-life photography, papier-mâché projects, macramé, woodcut printing using hand-rolling inkers called brayers—all those crafty things I already knew how to do. I made them design a batik pattern using graph paper—if you can imagine such a thing! Then they had to enlarge and transfer it to their muslin and start the waxing and dyeing processes. Batik takes forever, which was just what the doctor ordered—something to make the year in the high school art class pass quickly.

The only complaint I ever heard from the high school students concerned using graph paper. They thought it was too much work and wanted to draw their designs freehand. Too bad, so sad—it was my way (the longer way) or the highway. Now that I'm older and wiser, I'd let them. At the time, in my third year of teaching, I was just trying to keep my head above water and survive for nine months. I knew I was leaving in June for bigger and better places. If I could just get through nine months in the frozen, remote north, I'd be on my way.

Newfoundland was considered a remote, unpleasant, hardship assignment; therefore, it was a one-year area. One-year areas were for idiots like me who, while being interviewed, swore they'd go anywhere in the world! We were paid a 10 percent differential, which means 10 percent more than our base salary to finish the year. We were given a "free" trip home on a navy cargo plane once per year, in June. Any other time, you paid for your commercial flight, provided you could get to the international airport, which was one hour away in good weather. The weather was never good.

Why was I depressed? I had never been isolated before, and not only was I in a frigid northern land with icebergs, but I lived in a building with the same people I ate breakfast and dinner with, the same people who got together once a month for a party at the Officers Club (The O' Club was a dining and party club for civilians and officers. Officers were graduates of universities. The Enlisted Club was a dining and party club for the enlisted personnel without degrees. However, many enlisted receive their degrees during their time in the service. Universities, such as the University of Maryland, send professors from the States to teach. Many officers receive second Bachelors or Master's degrees while in the service.), the same people who were in the bowling league, and so forth. It became quite evident that certain personalities thrived in one-year scenarios. I didn't. I didn't like having to be friends with people I did not want to be friends with at all.

The people who loved Newfoundland were the men who loved to hunt and fish. It was an outdoor wonderland for them. The rest of us made do. I learned how to bowl, how to pour slip and paint ceramics, play bridge, and drink. Pouring slip is fundamental to casting molds of ceramics. Once your mold is dry, it's baked in a kiln and is then ready for painting. The only habit I've kept since Newfoundland is drinking. I haven't bowled, made anything from a mold, or played bridge since—and I haven't missed any of those pastimes either.

We did have parties in the BOQ area. There were the Rooper-Dooper Pong Parties, usually while watching Canadian curling matches or soccer matches on TV. RD Pong is just like Ping Pong, except when you miss a shot; then you have to guzzle your lovely glass of minty green RD. (I've included the recipe for those of you who are risk takers.) On other occasions we'd play tiddlywinks or pickup sticks—anything to offset the boredom of an isolated one-year assignment.

The first month I was in country, a friend decided we were going camping while the weather was still reasonably warm. The guys were in charge of the equipment, and my friend was in charge of the food. I was only going along for the adventure because I'd never camped out before. She and I went to the commissary to buy the food. She decided we'd buy ready-to-eat meals (MREs). That was about all she did buy, except for bagels and cream cheese for breakfast. You can imagine the swearing that broke out when the navy guys found out what was for dinner. If you've never had an MRE, ask one of your military friends to bring you one—you are in for a treat.

We always had blizzards, but one in particular will always remain with me. It lasted three days. After it was over, we woke up to the sun shining; the cars we'd parked in the lot below our residence were now sitting in the middle of the parking lot, completely blown out of their slots. Snow had drifted everywhere in the wind. Everyone lived on the base, so during snowstorms life went on as usual. School in Newfoundland was never canceled due to the weather. DoDDS teachers are just like mailmen—we deliver whether it's raining, sleeting, hailing, or snowing.

I remember driving to St. John's for a weekend getaway. We shopped during the day and met at a restaurant on the wharf for dinner. Russian ships were in port, along with all the other usual ships. Russian food was listed on the menus, as well as all the fish you could ever wish for. We saw icebergs in St. John's Bay on one of our trips. I didn't appreciate it at the time, but a lot of what you read in the social studies books about Nova Scotia and Newfoundland was there for us to experience.

Another weekend a girlfriend and I were planning to visit one of the French islands. This is the same teacher who drove to St. John's each week to take the rest of the classes she needed to finish her Master's degree. Weather was her only hassle. She drove no matter what the weather; sometimes she had to spend the night with another student and drive back to the navy base bright and early the next morning before her classes started. She had been hired with the understanding that she finished the degree within a year. She finished those two or three classes before school was out in June and trans-ferred to Europe too.

On this particular weekend we took my car, which I'd never driven off the base, but the car's previous owner swore it was great for driving to St. John's. But instead we were heading in the opposite direction from St. John's to catch a ferry over to the French island. I'll bet its previous owner had never traveled that route. The narrow road went up and down high, steep hills. Toward the end of the trip, the car simply died about two-thirds of the way up a very steep hill. We sat there for a few minutes, not daring to look at each other. We stewed internally. I let the engine rest five minutes and tried to start it again. It didn't start.

What were we going to do? We were in the middle of nowhere. Cell phones hadn't been invented yet; there were no garages; no other cars were out on the road on a Saturday bright with sunshine. The worst part was we hadn't told anyone where we were going. Another five minutes went by. I tried starting it again, and this time the old Toyota started, and it ran well for the rest of the weekend! We enjoyed our French island complete with French food until we left on Sunday. Since my time in Newfoundland, my husband and I have bought a lot of Toyotas.

That year of eating breakfast and dinner with everyone contributed to my love affair with cooking. Some of us started skipping the group meals to cook upstairs in the BOQ room or illegally in our rooms. I collected some great recipes that year. My husband loves them all, so we serve them a lot to relatives and friends and make them for teacher parties. Most of the recipes were just word of mouth and never written down until recently. They're included in the book. The only recipe I did not include from my year in Newfoundland was the "hamburger soup" my MRE-buying friend made up. It went over almost as well with the guys as the MRE dinners had!

Sometime in May I got my transfer to Germany. I was happy to leave my first assignment in June. My principal told me to just leave; he would pack out my household goods for me. I got a flight from St. John's to Montreal. After spending three days exploring that wonderful city, I boarded a plane back to Florida.

Grafenwoehr, or Graf, is an army training post one hour northeast of Nuremberg; it was my home for the next four years. During my first year in Germany, I ran into two teachers and one navy guy who had been stationed in Argentia with me.

I've never been back to Newfoundland, but when the school closed, I received an invitation to attend the closing ceremonies. I would have gone, of course, if Uncle Sam had given me a ticket on a military hop. I didn't receive one, and I wasn't surprised! Nothing comes free from Uncle Sam.

Rooper-Doopers

This recipe was shared with the personnel assigned to Argentia, Newfoundland, Canada, by a navy ensign in 1972. It's been taken around the world many times in the decades since then by many different men and women.

Remember, a little goes a long way; if you want a hangover, drink more than two! It's a pretty minty green color when ready to drink. Don't let that pretty shade of mint fool you.

Ingredients:
Mix equal amounts of each in a covered container; a mayonnaise jar works well:
    gin
    vodka
    crème de menthe
    crème de cacao
    cherry brandy

Directions:
Pour mixture into a glass until glass is about 1/3 full.

Pour milk into mixture until glass is about 2/3 full. Stir.

Add ice cubes. Now your Rooper-Dooper should be a pretty minty green!

Enjoy, if you dare!
*It makes no difference the brand of alcohol or the kind of milk. It will have the same effect on you whether you use skim, regular, or nonfat milk. I store leftovers in the fridge.

Confetti Casserole

This is an old farmer's recipe. I'm continually adding to it to make it better. If you use ground turkey, you might want to add some sage or chicken spices to it.

Preheat oven to 375 F.

Ingredients
    1 pound ground beef or ground sirloin
    1 small onion, chopped
    1 clove garlic, chopped
    3 ounces cream cheese
    1 tablespoon brown sugar
    4 ounces tomato sauce
    1 can mixed veggies or frozen, drained
    1 teaspoon dry mustard
    5 large biscuits; canned work well

Directions
Fry beef with chopped onion and garlic. Drain fat.

Add the cream cheese, brown sugar, and tomato sauce.

Stir until cheese melts.

Add mixed veggies. Stir and pour into 3-quart casserole. Cover and bake 30 minutes or until bubbly.

Place biscuits on top and adjust oven temperature and continue baking according to biscuit directions.

Jewish Chicken

This recipe came word of mouth from another resident of the mess hall/BOQ. I've often wondered why it's named Jewish Chicken; my Jewish friends haven't solved the mystery yet. Extra sauce can be frozen. I usually put all of it on the chicken. My husband's poker buddies love the sweet sauce! If you double the amount of chicken, double the sauce ingredients too. The best Jewish Chicken I've ever served was cooked inside a covered gas grill in Adana, Turkey, when the electricity went off during the baking process!

Preheat oven to 375 F.

Ingredients
> 4 chicken breasts with skin and bones

Sauce: 8-ounce bottle French dressing
> 1 package dried onion soup mix
> 1 can cranberry sauce with whole berries

Directions
Mix French dressing, dry onion soup mix, and cranberry sauce in a large bowl.

Place chicken breasts in baking dish, skin side down. Scoop a heaping tablespoon sauce on top of each chicken breast. Bake for 30 minutes.

Turn breasts over and add sauce to top side. Bake for another 30 minutes or until bubbly hot and brown on top.

Rose Porter

Russian Chicken

This was also passed around the BOQ in Argentia.

Ingredients
    8-ounce bottle or homemade Russian dressing
    1 package dry onion soup
    8-ounce jar peach or apricot preserves
    4 chicken breasts with skin

Directions

Mix Russian dressing, dry onion soup mix, and preserves in a large bowl.

Place chicken breasts in baking dish, skin side down. Scoop a heaping tablespoon sauce on top of each chicken breast.

Bake for 30 minutes at 375 F. Turn breasts over and add sauce to top side. Bake for another 30 minutes until bubbly hot and brown on top.

Wine Marinade
for
Beef Shish Kebob

Marinade Ingredients
    ½ cup dry white wine
    ½ cup ketchup
    1 tablespoon prepared mustard
    1 tablespoon Worcestershire sauce
    1 clove garlic, minced
    ½ teaspoon dried rosemary
    2 tablespoons cider vinegar
    2 tablespoons brown sugar
    1 pound sirloin, cut into 1½ inch pieces

Directions
Mix all sauce ingredients.

Cut sirloin into chunks and place in a plastic container with lid.
Pour sauce over meat, making sure both sides are covered with sauce. Place container in freezer for one week.

Thaw meat and pierce with skewers. Add raw vegetables if you wish.

Grill. Brush with marinade. Serve with leftover marinade.

The marinade and beef are easily adapted for large groups. Just double all ingredients. Freezing is essential for tender, flavorful meat.

Rose Porter

CHAPTER 3

1973–1977
Grafenwoehr, Germany

It was a sunny day in early August when the military plane landed in Frankfurt, Germany. Lots of teachers arrived to start the new school year in Europe. We were loaded onto military buses and taken to Wiesbaden, where we spent the night and completed lots of paperwork. The next day we entered buses going to different cities. I was on the bus to Nuremberg. At Nuremberg, three of us rode in a military taxi for our final drive.

We arrived at the school in Graf and met our principal, who became, and remains, my very favorite boss in the whole world. He and his wife welcomed us to Graf, took us to another teacher's house for a home-cooked meal, and got us settled in the local hotel.

Our welcome to our new school environment was the best we could ever have wished for. The next morning we started looking for apartments. We soon decided we had done enough walking and bought Peugeot bikes for transportation.

When school started, we were still eating our meals out. To this day I cannot eat green peas, mainly because the Officers Club served them every day. During the first month we all bought cars, and exactly one month after arriving in Graf, the three of us moved into an apartment in a nearby village. Then we started cooking at home. No more green peas for us!

We learned from the military guys that the army discouraged wearing jeans in the villages. The reason was the Germans didn't wear jeans, and their custom was to dress up when leaving the privacy of their homes. Dressing appropriately was a challenge for us in the beginning. We had to buy tailored slacks, which were a difficult thing to find. The Base Exchange (BX) did not offer the options it does today; there was no Internet, and the mail system was slower than Christmas.

We soon found out that the sunny weather that had greeted us on our arrival in Frankfurt was a fluke of nature. Germany turned out to be rainy, overcast, and dreary much of the time. We endured lots of snow in Grafenwoehr, but in the four years I taught there school was never closed because of it.

CHAPTER 4

Labor Day Weekend, 1973
Vienna, Austria

OUR FIRST SCHOOL HOLIDAY WAS LABOR DAY.

Because we walked over to the Officers Club every day for lunch, we made friends with the other single civilian and military types. One of the army captains was moving to another facility at the end of September. His idea of heaven was to take the train from Weiden, the closest town with a major *bahnhof* (train station), to Regensburg and transfer to a boat that would cruise down the Danube River to Vienna. He planned to fulfill his dream over the three-day weekend. Sounds great, doesn't it? We thought so, too, and we invited ourselves to go along with him. I don't think it was his idea of a good time, but he agreed that we could go. His only stipulation was that he would be the tour boss, and he got to tell us what to do. He would not allow us to slow him down and keep him from fulfilling his dream. We agreed. It was probably the talk of the post—one guy traveling with three young girls!

We didn't know him very well when we started out Friday night. By the time we returned Monday night, we knew more than we'd ever wished to know about anyone. The man never sat at a table to eat a meal. His idea of food was to buy a pretzel or a banana from a cart on the street. He walked us everywhere. We *never* took public transportation in Vienna. We walked miles and miles. Our tour guide had found a "hotel" in his *Europe on $5 a Day* "bible," which he carried around the way girls carry purses, quoting information about the sights from it. He was never without it.

Our hotel room was a dump on the third floor of an old house. He and the old lady who ran the boarding house left the three of us in our room, and they continued on upstairs to his room. We didn't see him again until breakfast the next morning. Breakfast in those days was bread or *brotchen* (hard rolls), butter, and jam, with coffee or tea. We compared notes on our rooms during breakfast. Our captain had a wrought-iron security-type door in front of his wooden door. Once the old lady locked him in, he was in to stay! She opened the guard door again the next morning. What a hoot! It's a good thing we didn't have a fire during the night.

It was cold during the nights, but the furnace didn't seem to be turned on. I guess that could have been a blessing even though we were freezing! A fire in that old house would have roared through it, trapping our captain and maybe the three of us. Europeans didn't turn on the heat until October 15, and they turned it off again April 15—a cost-saving habit of people who had too many taxes to pay and not enough money.

Bread was our main meal, three times a day, until we returned to the base. We had eaten bread on the boat, bread on the run while we were touring around, and now there was more bread for breakfast. When we returned to Weiden late Monday night, our tour guide decided that we should stop in a great restaurant he knew about before driving back to the post. At that time, it served great German food. The building was beautifully decorated with pewter, lace, and all the usual German trimmings. We were so happy to finally sit down and eat a hot meal with real meat and potatoes. But guess what? We couldn't eat. Our stomachs had shrunk from not eating for three days. We sat and just looked at the delicious food while our captain consumed everything in sight.

After we recovered from our "holiday," we laughed and laughed within the confines of our apartment. We could never say much during the remaining lunches at the club before our new friend and tour guide left Graf and moved to Frankfurt at the end of September.

One of the first things I learned in Germany was how to drink beer. At home the drink of choice was always unsweetened iced tea. Don't go looking for iced tea in Europe; you won't find it. (Nowadays, you'll see iced tea in small bottles, but it's not American. It's sweetened with chemicals and isn't worth the price they ask for it.) Our choices at the time were carbonated water, Coke, juice, beer, and wine. Beer was cheaper and the glasses were larger, so beer became my new drink of choice. On our cruise down the Danube, I discovered beer and bread can fill you up and keep your stomach from growling.

Later in the school year, the three of us returned to that restaurant so that we could finally say we'd eaten a meal there. The restaurant is still in Weiden. Years later I returned to look for it and found that it was no longer German; it was Italian. The last time we were in Weiden, we stopped for lunch and had a great Greek meal. The building is probably seven hundred years old, and its present owners are still dishing out great food.

❧ CHAPTER 5 ❧
Columbus Day Weekend 1973
Prague

OUR NEXT VACATION WAS COLUMBUS DAY WEEKEND. WE BOOKED A BUS TOUR TO Prague. We were very excited. We piled into one of our three cars and drove to Frankfurt to catch the bus that Friday night. The bus driver drove through the night; some of the scenery looked familiar, but it was dark. We arrived at the border between Germany and East Germany, where we sat for a long time before the bus tour passed the guards' inspection. Then we continued on through the night toward Prague.

The tour was a cheap one, and the hotel reflected just how cheap it was. We had to walk up a grand staircase to the first floor and then regular stairs up to our room on the fourth floor. None of us were willing stair climbers, and we learned really fast to decide our day's schedule before we went down for breakfast. We toured the old city, took in some local night life, and ate some unappetizing food. It was cold, so when we ran out of energy to walk, we hopped a tram to nowhere in particular. We rode for a couple of hours, seeing the old city without benefit of a tour guide. We were happy to leave on the long bus trip back to Frankfurt.

When we stopped at the border, the guards decided to check the baggage. I guess they were looking for inappropriate souvenirs that would be considered contraband; icons from the churches were a favorite item. We were lucky. Our three suitcases were chosen for the honor. They took out all the dirty clothes; our dirty underwear was waved around with gusto amid the chuckles of the guards. We three were not smiling, but our fellow travelers thought it was funny.

We crossed the border in daylight this time and realized that we were about thirty minutes from Graf. You could not catch a bus en route to a tour city; you had to pick it up at the official bus stops. We could have simply driven the car to Weiden, but because of the rules, we ended up making a very long, three-hour trip to and from our pickup point, which would be totally unnecessary after the Berlin Wall came down on November 9, 1989. Reunification Day is now a highly celebrated holiday in Germany, especially in Berlin.

CHAPTER 6

Veterans Day 1973
Berlin, West Germany

THE THREE OF US FLEW TO BERLIN OVER VETERANS DAY WEEKEND. OF COURSE, WE had to drive to Frankfurt to catch the plane, not to the local airport in Nuremberg. We stayed in a very nice hotel, compliments of an American Express tour, which was the local tour company at that time. We took the bus tour to East Berlin, along with service men and women in uniform. It was interesting, a little scary, and freezing cold! We saw old, drab buildings, but there was no shopping to speak of. We visited the Brandenburg Gate where President Kennedy gave his famous speech in 1963 "Ich bin ein Berliner." It's the same Gate where later President Reagan told the Russian Premier Gorbachev to open the Gate and tear down the wall. It did come down on 9 November 1989, but it wasn't legal until 3 October 1990. We took a tour of the Egyptian Museum and saw the bust of Nefertiti for the first time. The Pergamon Museum was behind the wall in the Russian Zone so we didn't get to see all the treasures it holds.

We still did not know how to read a German menu, but that never stopped us from eating in restaurants. We found one advertised in a local publication for visitors to Berlin and decided to give it a try. Each of us ordered a different entree. The pickiest eater of the group ordered beef tartare; none of us knew what it was, but it sounded good. We'd been out most of the day, walking in Germany's typical rainy November weather, and we were cold, tired, and hungry. When our meals came, two of us started digging in. The third member of our group just sat and looked at her meal. My husband says beef tartare, which is raw steak ground up like hamburger, is great. I've never had the desire to be that brave.

We flew back home the next day and were happy we'd seen the Berlin from our history books.

✦ CHAPTER 7 ✦

Junk and Crystal

WE'D LEARNED FROM OTHERS ON THE BASE THAT BAYREUTH WAS A GREAT PLACE TO shop for furniture. There was a junk store called Harry's that had lots of good, cheap junk for sale. The bedroom sets, a favorite of the American women, had marble tops. Ladies would drive up in the largest mode of transportation they could find and haul huge pieces back to the post.

My friends and I went for the sewing machine bases, to be matched with the marble from a dresser. We'd buy the machine, remove it right there in the store, and leave the machine for Harry to resell. The wrought-iron base plus the marble dresser top became a sought-after antique. I still have two, and they're great for just about any purpose: hall table, TV table, dining table for two, and more. They're really worth their weight at Christmas time because they can accommodate lots of attractive European and Israeli items. Our olivewood nativity scene goes well anywhere we put it, but a wrought-iron and marble table is my favorite.

If you are interested in crystal, then Weiden is the place to go. When the crystal artisans and their families escaped from East Germany, they settled in the Weiden area. Nachtmann is still very popular; if a crystal wine glass is broken, take it to Nachtmann, and they'll turn it into a bell for you. You can special-order items—they'll ship to you, or you can return and pick it up yourself.

We sometimes drove to the border towns to go shopping on weekends; I bought my first piece of Russian porcelain during one of those Saturday trips. People escaping the East would come through a village and sell their belongings. The items they sold were not for sale in the typical German stores because they weren't available for import. I had no idea of the history of the porcelain, but I loved the hand-painted blue and white pieces. I ended up with five different pieces from those trips. I even found a vase, which I took with me to Seoul, where a Korean electrician made it into a lamp. We still use it.

The bazaars run by the Officers Wives Club (OWC) in Europe are great places to buy items from all over the world. The OWC makes a profit from hosting the events, but the money goes to the schools or to scholarships for students. Vendors from all over visit the army posts and air force bases two or three times per year. We bought Christmas presents at the September bazaar to ship home in November. It was one-stop shopping. They sold Christmas ornaments and eggs for Easter trees, along with bunnies and the usual Easter animals. We could find leather from Italy and sometimes Turkey; fur coats from Italy, Korea, or Russia; heavy ski sweaters from Norway and Finland; Bavarian leather breeches and women's dirndls; Polish pottery, and crystal from Weiden, just to name a few.

One of my treasures is a nutcracker bar stool which I'd bought at one of the bazaars. Later Frank and I drove to the factory which was located in an extensive forest somewhere close to Stuttgart. Our trip was before GPS, so we had to find our way the old-fashioned way; we got so lost looking for the factory that we stopped at the *polizei* (police station) and asked for directions. The police decided to drive us to the factory, which was easier than giving directions. We were definitely in the boondocks of Germany.

We also asked them for help in finding an hotel for the night. It was winter and our light was fading fast. We didn't want to try driving through the forest again without some sunlight. So after ordering our nutcrackers, we drove to an old, old hotel, the only one in the area. The food was typical: schnitzel (a breaded and fried pork steak), fries, and salad. The bed was older than Christmas, lumpy, and uncomfortable. The room felt as if there was no heat, and the toilet was down the hall. Another room contained the bathtub, and all were shared by everybody on that floor.

It was so cold our two miniature schnauzers dug themselves under the covers to keep warm; Missy put her head on Frank's pillow and slept the night away. Cinder was better behaved but still slept under the covers, which kept me warmer. As you can imagine, the price for food and the room was the cheapest we'd encountered, but we would have gladly paid double just to have heat! We still consider that hotel the worst we've ever stayed at in all our travels around Europe.

CHAPTER 8

Spring Break 1974
Athens, Greece

THE FIRST SPRING BREAK, EIGHT OF US GIRLS DECIDED WE NEEDED SOME FUN IN THE sun. Several of the girls were teachers at Vilseck, the neighboring DoDDS school. Neither of my roommates opted to go with us. One had to save money to pay her state income tax, and the other was shopping around for a place to live in her transfer city of choice. One of the girls at Vilseck organized us. We booked a cheap flight and an even cheaper hotel in Athens. I doubt if stars had ever been a goal of the hotel owner. That's how cheap it was. The bathtub was a sight to behold; I never saw anything like it again until my husband and I moved to Okinawa. No tour of Athens was included. We were roughing it, paying as things came up. Breakfast was included; such as it was. But we were in heaven! Forget Vienna. Athens is heaven on Earth.

We took the city bus out to Glyfada Beach each morning, hid behind the boulders until the sun was really hot, and then stripped down to our swimsuits. It might have been spring break, but Mother Nature controlled us. We spent late afternoons and evenings seeing the sights and looking for a suitable (cheap) restaurant for dinner. We ate moussaka every night. It was the only Greek food word we knew, and it was cheap! It was always made with potatoes, not eggplant, which helped to keep it cheap. We went to the Plaka one night for the dinner show. In return for the price of dinner and drinks, you got to watch the dancing free of charge. The real reason we wanted to go was to watch them breaking the plates during the dancing. We weren't disappointed. It's something you need to see once.

Riding in a taxi at night was an experience of a lifetime. Taxi drivers drove with their lights off. The taxis were old, dented, and very uncomfortable, but cheap. Late one night we decided to take the bus from Athens to Delphi; it left at zero dark thirty in the morning so we took taxis to the bus station. We left so early we had no breakfast. Well, the bus ride lasted more than six hours. We were starving by the time we arrived, and I don't remember actually sitting down and eating. I'm sure we did; we probably had moussaka again, but we were more interested in shopping.

Flokati rugs are a great buy in Greece. Silk batiks are popular also. I still have both the Flokati and the batik I bought in Delphi. The wool comes from the Flokati sheep, which are raised all over Greece. You must wash the rugs in cold water and let them air-dry. I did it myself only once. After that I hauled it to the on-base laundry for someone stronger than me to haul out of the washtub. Now I take it to the German cleaners—even better!

The Delphi salesman mailed the Flokati to the apartment in Eschenbach. It took two or three weeks, but it arrived. I never doubted that it would. Ignorance is certainly bliss. I would probably never have anything mailed back home now, but in my early days I believed anything and everything was possible.

Vilseck's drama queen had joined our trip. During one unforgettable meal she got a horrified look on her face, proceeded to stand up, and then crouched on her chair seat. The rest of us were totally confused. She didn't scream, yell, or speak; she just pointed dramatically. Over in the corner crouched a tiny mouse. She got the laugh she wanted, but we had created a monster.

All of us took a sunset bus tour to Cape Sounion to see the Greek temple of Poseidon. There were no safety railings on the road around the curvy cliff leading to Cape Sounion. All of a sudden there was a piercing shriek behind us. The drama queen had just noticed where the rest of us were looking—down the side of the cliff, where the bus would end up if the driver lost control of the bus for some reason.

King Aegeus had leaped to his death off this cliff, which resulted in the sea becoming known as the Aegean Sea. Lord Bryon, one of my favorite poets from high school, had visited the site and scratched his name onto the temple. Little did he know that young, and probably older, ladies would travel the world looking for his initials. He's not as famous as Napoleon, but English students know him well.

Our trip to Athens would not have been complete without a cruise to the islands. We visited Aegina, Mykonos, and Hydra. We took a standard (cheap) tour aboard a ferry to three of the islands. The main part of the town of Aegina had many seafood restaurants. We could eat, drink, and shop for treasures there. Mykonos is famous for the windmills. Hydra had donkeys for rent to take you up to the cultural site. Guess which one of us decided to have a donkey ride? You guessed it. The drama queen kept us entertained until she and the donkey were out of sight.

Athens was so much fun at spring break that several of us went back in June right after school was out; this time we took some married teachers with us. They left their husbands at home so they could go with "the girls." It wasn't as much fun because of the extremely hot weather. Plus the drama queen had decided she needed to go home to see her friends and relatives in the States instead of returning.

We walked from air-conditioned stores to air-conditioned restaurants just to keep the temperature at bay. We ate a lot of cold watermelon that trip. The married ones loved the trip. Shoes were the hot item in June, and we bought lots of sandals. Athens got their tourist dollars out of us, and we had a great time in the bazaar bargaining for copper.

One of the single teachers later married one of the army captains from Vilseck. The ceremony was held in the chapel with their local friends. After the ceremony, the bride and groom rode off in a tank borrowed from his unit. I haven't seen anything like that since. In Germany couples had to go to the local marriage office to begin the legal paperwork. Then they'd get married on post for their local friends, fly home to the States, and get married again for the families—one legal marriage with two ceremonies to make everyone happy. It's another reason DoDDS teachers earned their paychecks. Who else had to pay for two ceremonies and two receptions after they'd already paid the legal fees?

I've lost track of how many times I've returned to Greece. Once there was a DoDDS school there, but I never wanted to live with that heat. Besides, in the old transfer system, you had to transfer to the worst places in the world in order to leave your current assignment. No one considered Athens among the worst places.

❋ CHAPTER 9 ❋
Year Two: 1974–1975
To Russia, With Love

IN MY SECOND YEAR IN GRAFENWOEHR, I HAD ONLY ONE ROOMMATE. THE THIRD one gave up on the quiet farming community and transferred to the big city of Wurzburg. She became a season ticket–holder to both the opera and symphony. She had always been a third-grade teacher, but our wonderful boss talked her into becoming a first-grade teacher; she didn't really have a choice, because that's where the opening was.

Transferring DoDDS teachers have an idea of their new grade level but once you get to your new duty station, the principal always has the final word. You can be placed in any grade for which you are certified. You could arrive thinking you're a new third grade teacher only to find out that your assignment has been switched to fifth grade. There are many reasons for changes: higher student enrollment in a grade level, having more experience in another grade level versus another "new" teacher who has only taught one level. That's one reason DoDDS teachers became DoDDS teachers; they are the best of the thousands who apply each year. You need to be flexible, versatile, and willing to change without a tense argument, or your life won't be a happy one. At least, that was the criteria when I was hired. I still believed that when I retired, even with the presence by then of the teachers union.

The second year meant a new chaplain, new young officers, and new young parents. The students were great, just as the students in Florida had been. The parents were wonderful.

During spring break, a Vilseck friend and I took a tour to Moscow, Leningrad, and Helsinki. I borrowed a fake fur from our new Mrs. Chaplain and enjoyed the trip. It was cold, but I've been colder since then.

We had a mandatory military briefing before we left. Consequently, we were expecting Russian spies everywhere we toured. We checked our hotel room for bugs. We refused to say our true feelings unless we were in a public place. We were great representatives for the United States.

If didn't take us long to decide that our room *was* bugged. We decided to investigate a strange bump under our rug. Halfway through our investigation we had an epiphany. The bump we were unscrewing attached the chandelier in the room below us!

Years later, a friend from Taegu shared his Russian story. He met Liz Taylor when he was visiting Russia. She and her entourage were staying in the same hotel as he, and they were very happy to see and talk with another American. What a great story! We met no such celebrity on our trip.

We visited the Metro Museum, which was built by Stalin; he used the subways for bomb shelters and as a safe storage facility for the treasures he stole. We went to the Bolshoi Ballet and to the Moscow Circus. We shopped in Gum's Department Store. A trip to Moscow is never complete without a visit to St. Basil's, the Kremlin, or Red Square. Our tour also included a very old Jewish cemetery on the coldest day of our tour in Moscow. There are many other sites to visit on a tour of Moscow, but we only saw the most famous ones.

All the meals were included; the lunches and dinners were three-course meals, and not Russian food; since we tourists had come from Germany, we were served German food.

There is no other word to describe Russia except that it was depressing. My most vivid memory of that trip was the dirty windows. Both the government buildings and the hi-rise apartments had filthy looking windows. It was cold, overcast, and dirty, and the citizens appeared to be deprived. You could see long lines of people standing outside food stores, waiting to buy some food for their families. Food sold out quickly so people didn't mind waiting for their time to enter the store. No one wanted to go home empty-handed especially with many relatives living in your small apartment. There were some cars, but they were Russian and small. I didn't realize how dreary Russia really was until we flew from Moscow to Helsinki. The sun was shining when we landed. The windows in the airport were spotless. The people were smiling and appeared happy to be alive. We started smiling again. That's when I realized we hadn't smiled for five days.

Shopping in the Helsinki airport was fantastic. We were finally back to normal again. Thanks to the atmosphere in the Scandinavian airport, I started an expensive new habit. I started buying clothes in the countries I visited. I came home with a beautiful turquoise poncho, which I still wear today. It will never wear out, thanks to the Finnish workmanship.

My last roommate met her husband that year, and they moved back to CONUS—the Continental United States. Later we called it "CONUS, that mythical island south of Guam." I think that expression came later, with my air force husband.

Rose Porter

✦ CHAPTER 10 ✦
Year Three: 1975–1976
Israel

SCHOOL YEAR (SY) AUGUST 1974-JUNE 1975 ENDED WITH SUMMER VACATION AND SY 1975-76 began with a new group of students in late August. That November our chapel helped sponsor a tour to the Holy Land during Thanksgiving week. One of the young army guys, a teacher from Nuremberg, and I joined the tour. The weather was great, just cool enough for a light jacket. We visited all the religious sites, stayed in newly finished hotels, ate lamb that was so very bad that it took twenty years before I could try eating it again. I've forgotten the name of the tiny town, but we checked into our hotel which was recently finished, had dinner, and retired for the night. The next morning I tried to go down for breakfast, but the door would not open. I did everything to open that silly door in our new recently finished hotel. Luckily, there was a telephone which worked, so the kid from the desk came up and rescued me. He couldn't figure out what was wrong with the lock, but I carried my suitcase down with me. I wasn't going to take a chance on it locking me in again.

Since we were participating in a chaplains' tour, participants were given the opportunity to be baptized in the Sea of Galilee. When we arrived at the Dead Sea, participants from other groups were being baptized in the salty water.

We stayed in a very nice hotel in Tel Aviv, right on the beach. We'd never seen the Mediterranean; of course, we had to take a swim! It didn't matter that it was late November, and we were wearing jackets during the day. We rendezvoused in the lobby at five thirty that morning. Once we got outside in the cold, two of us came to our senses; only the bravest went into the water—the trained army soldier!

We couldn't pass up a chance to visit the King David Hotel; after all, that's where all the rich and famous people stayed or went to see Frank Sinatra perform. I did see one famous Broadway actor. Robert Morse won a *Tony* for his role as businessman J. Pierrepont Finch in *How to Succeed in Business Without Really Trying.* Mr. Morse looked right at me, realized I recognized him, and turned away to make a quick retreat. I'm not into autographs, so he would have been safe from me, but little did he know.

We tried to get lots of pictures of the locals, but in Israel, you need their permission.

The people possessing the local color who were worthy of photographs wouldn't allow it. They believe a photograph would steal part of their soul, so there were no pictures unless you sneaked them. If you got caught sneaking one, they threw rocks at you or the bus.

Everywhere we toured we saw young teenage boys in military uniforms. They stood around holding loaded Uzis that were almost as big as they were. It was scary—not a sight you wanted to see too often.

The Israelis were friendly and let us bargain with them for kilims and head coverings. We bought menorahs and candles for Hanukkah activities back at school. All of us took a piece of Israel home in the form of a rock. We left Israel with our skin a little darker in color than when we entered and with lots of slides to prove our visit really happened. It was a great week.

After returning to Graf, I was asked to share my slides with the chapel members. Most people had a visit to Israel on their wishlist. Nowadays the chaplins no longer support a chapel tour to Israel. The terrorists have made a lot of great trips no longer feasible due to safety issues.

❧ CHAPTER 11 ❧
December 1975
An African Safari:
Kenya, Tanzania, and Uganda

THAT SAME YEAR FOUR OF US FLEW TO AFRICA FOR A SAFARI DURING OUR CHRISTMAS break. We had to prepare for the trip months in advance. We needed certain shots and boosters. Malaria was a big concern. One of the teachers made an appointment, paid his dollar, and asked a doctor for the appropriate malaria prophylactic. The sweet young doctor, just out of med school and paying off his education by serving in the army, wanted to help us out. He opened up his "drug tome" and picked the medicine we needed. He wrote prescriptions for all four of us so that we wouldn't have to bother him again. We were overjoyed. We had the prescriptions and didn't have to race over to the dispensary (small hospital) after school in order to get a prescription before closing time.

The pills were big brown horse pills. We were to start taking them two weeks before getting on the plane and continue them for two weeks after we returned to school. Being the good examples of DoDDS teachers that we were, we followed his directions like bees swarming to pollen.

We landed at the international airport in Nairobi, Kenya, spent the night in the four-star Hilton Hotel, and flew to Tanzania the next morning to start our safari. We had splurged on an expensive tour, the only way to travel in Africa. We started in Tanzania with the Masai warriors; we stayed in very nice tourist camps, flew by private plane from one safari camp to another, slept under mosquito nets, rode around in a Land Rover, and had a glorious time. We all bought our obligatory safari hats to deflect the sun, used suntan lotion religiously, and took our medicine.

Day three was the turning point. My roommate went to take a bath and passed out in the tub. I went racing for our tour guide. Our African/British guide decided it was just too much excitement, the change of climate, different food, and so forth. My roommate argued that it was the malaria pills. She stopped taking them.

The next morning at breakfast we found out that one of the guys had been affected by the big brown horse pills too; every time he stood up, he'd get dizzy, as if he were going to pass out. After hearing the tub story, he also decided to stop taking the pills. Two of us were off the malaria prophylactic and two of us were still taking them. I was the third one to stop, a few days and two countries later.

We finished Tanzania and flew on to Kenya. I never saw any tanzanite while I was in Tanzania either; our safari occurred before the terrorists sold it to pay for their activities abroad. But we saw every animal you could wish to see on a safari in Kenya. We saw lots of babies too—hippos, elephants, rhinos, gazelles, lion cubs, zebras, antelopes, giraffes, dick-dicks. One night we were in the dining room, and a waiter came by and whispered to someone at the table. A panther was feeding at the riverbank below the lodge. We were up in seconds, trying like crazy to see or to take a picture. We all said we saw it, but I'm not sure any of us really did. Our Christmas dinner was served at one of our overnight lodges. The turkey and dressing substitute must have been good because I don't even remember eating Christmas meals.

My Southern Baptist aunt used to talk about pink elephants. I thought she must have started drinking or something. She was exonerated on the safari because we actually saw pink elephants. Do you know why they're pink? As the water evaporates from the rivers, the riverbeds become wet red clay. Elephants like to roll in the clay to keep their skin cool. Hence, pink elephants!

After flying around Kenya, we were nearing the end of our safari. We still had Uganda on our itinerary. We'd see Victoria Falls, more animals, more interesting faces. We landed at Kampala Airport and got settled in our hotel. It was a nice place, but we were surprised to receive a visitor soon after we registered. A nice gentleman from the American Embassy came to tell us Uganda wasn't safe and to leave the country. We, of course, being poor schoolteachers who had splurged and saved our pennies for months to make this Christmas trip, told him, "No way, Jose." We had paid for three days in Uganda, and we were going to get our money's worth. Boy, were we stupid!

We were the last tour group that had been allowed into the country; then the American Embassy put Uganda on the official watch/no approval list for travelers. If you're a government employee and visit such a country, you could possibly lose your job. It would all depend on the resulting international incident. If an employee of our embassy came to see me at a hotel today, I'd be on the next plane back to a safer location. But not back in December 1975. Those were my dumber days. If you remember, the Israelis made a raid on the Entebbe Airport in July of 1976 to rescue more than a hundred Jews from a hostage situation. The movie *Victory at Entebbe* was made about it. Lots of big name actors, like Anthony Hopkins, Kirk Douglas, Burt Lancaster, Richard Dreyfuss, and Elizabeth Taylor starred in it.

We continued our safari, which meant getting up at five in the morning to drive out to see the animals while they were feeding. We'd return and have breakfast and relax until evening feeding time. We'd go out again, come back, and have dinner. It

Rose Porter

was during those last three days that I started feeling sick. After ten days in Africa, I wasn't too upset. I just slept my days away and skipped the morning and evening outings. Our last day culminated with a typical Ugandan barbecue for New Year's Eve. All afternoon they cooked rabbit and goat. The music was loud, but I didn't mind. I was too sick to care. It was about then that I quit taking the malaria horse pills. We packed up and left the next morning. I don't remember too much about the barbecue. I couldn't tell you whether the goat was good or not. I'm sure the rabbit was but I've had rabbit lots of time.

We got split up on the airplane; I sat behind my three friends. All I remember about the long flight home was sleeping; if I wasn't asleep, my head was pounding. When we got to Frankfurt, we started the long drive back to Graf. I slept until we arrived in Wurzburg for dinner. I ate something, got back in the car, and proceeded to sleep all the way to Vilseck, where I got into my orange VW Super Beetle and drove home to Graf.

The next morning I felt great. I got dressed and went to school. Things were back to normal. I think it was two days later that the shakes started. At first I thought I must be cold, so I put on my coat and walked around the classroom like that. Then I wised up. I wasn't cold. I left school and went to the dispensary. I saw another doctor, not the one who had prescribed the malaria pills. He didn't have a clue what my problem was, other than I'd been in Africa. He said I should expect some repercussions after fourteen days. I never understood the analogy. My stomach wasn't upset. I just had the shakes. The next morning I was fine. About two or three days later, I had the shakes again.

I told my wonderful boss I needed to drive to Nuremberg to the military hospital. I walked in without an appointment and asked to see a doctor. Lucky for me, the man I saw had spent some time in Vietnam. He listened to me talk for a few minutes and said I had malaria and that he'd do a blood test to prove it to me. I couldn't have malaria, I argued. I had taken those God-forsaken big brown horse pills for almost four weeks. I'd slept under a mosquito net every night.

Guess what? Those pills were the wrong ones! The real malaria prophylactic pill is tiny and white, and you take it once a week for about six weeks. The pills we had been prescribed by our young doctor in Graf were for someone who already had malaria.

The Nuremberg doctor gave me medicine that cured the symptoms. I was told that the malaria could come back, but if it didn't show up within a year, I would probably never have a reoccurrence. Because I've had malaria, I'm not allowed to give blood; whenever there's a blood drive; I have to tell them I've had malaria. Then I wait to see if they still want some. They've never been desperate enough for blood.

Malaria is transmitted by the anopheles mosquito. We slept under mosquito nets each night, and I can't remember getting a mosquito bite. It's a mystery why I was selected for the honor and my three friends were unaffected. The only good thing that came out of my experience is that I finally grew up and started questioning adults, especially doctors. Now when I get a diagnosis, I keep seeing doctors until at least two of them agree with the original one. It's a lot easier now that we can check information with the Internet.

Rose Porter

CHAPTER 12

February 1976
Skiing On the Zugspitz

AFTER OUR TRIP TO AFRICA, I DECIDED TO TRY SKIING. I TOOK A COUPLE OF WEEKEND skiing trips, including lessons. To make a long story short, I went to Garmisch one weekend with my expert skier friends. I was on the Zugspitz, which I shouldn't have been as a novice. I ended up skiing on ice, falling, and breaking my lower left leg in four places. The bindings on my rented skis didn't release.

I did suffer the break under the best of circumstances. A ski patrolman was sitting nearby, watching to see if I was going to get up. He skied over about the time I sat up and noticed my left leg facing left while my body was facing right. As he arrived by my side, I had just picked up my broken leg and turned it over so that it was facing right. Talk about being in shock! I remember doing it, but I felt no pain. He stayed with me until the rescue team put me into the ambulance. The doctor at the Garmisch Clinic took x-rays, said he wasn't touching me, and sent me in another ambulance to the hospital in Augsburg.

The military hospital in Augsburg had a great German doctor working in orthopedics. For the next week I thought I had dreamed the whole experience, right down to the leg cast. It wasn't until I was going home and he X-rayed my leg again that I realized it had been no dream. In my "dream" the doctor had sat me down in a chair. He and another guy picked up the chair and put it on top of the examination table. Then I was instructed to scoot to the edge of the chair and dangle my broken leg downward. I had been given a shot at the Garmisch clinic, so I was feeling no pain. I did what the doctor told me to do. He put on my cast, and then I was taken to a ward. I spent the next seven to ten days going to therapy and learning how to walk with crutches. The day before I was to leave, I had to get new X-rays. My bones weren't growing back together the correct way, so I needed some bone readjustment work. That time I was wide awake, with no painkillers.

My previous "dream" became reality. They sat me down in a chair, picked up the chair, placed it on the table, and cut off the old cast. Then the doctor started manipulating the broken bones by squeezing my leg. As he worked, he looked at the X-ray. When he was satisfied that the bones would grow back correctly, I got a new cast. Meanwhile, I was back in shock again. I found it extremely hard to believe my eyes. I couldn't believe broken legs were set in such a bizarre fashion. I have no idea if that was standard operating procedure. I really don't need or want to know.

The new cast worked, and I went back to school. My kids were great! As I became progressively stronger, they became progressively more active. I was teaching in a wheelchair until I got a walking cast. My boss traded cars with me so I could start driving myself to school. I didn't know that was against the German driving laws. Ignorance is, indeed, bliss. Up until the walking cast, I had been picked up each morning by a teacher friend; another went to the commissary for me. My landlord's wife became my *putzfrau*, or cleaning lady (there are benefits to having a broken limb), and I was well taken care of. You need friends if you're single in DoDDS. My walker was exchanged for a cane sometime in late April.

⇜ CHAPTER 13 ⇝

July 1976
Norway and the Fjords

JUNE ARRIVED. MOST OF THE STAFF WENT HOME FOR THE VACATION PERIOD. My girlfriend from the Africa trip and I decided to drive to Scandinavia to see the fjords. We packed our winter clothes into her cute little car and started off for the car ferry. We arrived in Lubeck late in the day and drove around looking for a pension or cheap (no-star) hotel.

We saw a building with a red door; it looked inviting. As we started walking up to the establishment to ask about a room, we noticed a large mirror in the middle of the red door. Our brains still didn't kick in. We opened the door and walked in. That's when we realized where we were! The scantily clad girls inside started shaking their heads furiously and laughing. We got the picture, walked out, and went into hysterics! We had just walked into a house of ill-repute, looking for a room for the night! Only in DoDDS will you hear stories like this.

We finally found a nice room for the night and an outdoor fair to investigate. We had bratwurst (spicy sausage) and pommes (french fries) for dinner, with cotton candy for dessert. The next morning we continued on our way and made it aboard the car ferry. It was our first time on a car ferry but loading the car was relatively easy. We drove off on the other side of the Baltic Sea while passengers who had walked on in Germany left by foot in Denmark. In July, while we walked from our hotel to Tivoli Gardens, I realized I was no longer limping and threw my cane away. If you like amusement parks, go toTivoli Gardens which opened for the first time in 1843. If you like concerts, then singers like Tony Bennett, Lady Gaga, and Elton John are performing in the summer of 2015 along with classical concerts. Discover Danish midsummer traditions and music by attending *Midsummer Night in Tivoli.*

We drove past the signs warning about reindeer crossing the road all the way up to Oslo. We left the car and then hopped a train to where we wanted to catch the cog train to the fjord. Then we bought a ticket on a ship and started sailing. It was freezing cold even in my warmest ski jacket. Along the way we docked at a hotel for the night and had a great salmon dinner. The next morning the ship continued through the fjords to Bergen. It was a wonderful experience, full of natural beauty, and all for the cheap price of a seat on a ship delivering supplies. No regular cruise ships were allowed on the route we took, and they still aren't. After arriving in Bergen, we took the train back to the car and drove home, but we didn't stop in Lubeck! It's a trip I want to repeat with my husband some July before we PCS (permanent change of station) back to the retirement home.

Some of the recipes I've collected and have been using since I left Grafenwoehr in 1977 follow. They are all delicious and should be enjoyed by all my readers. *Bon appetit*!

Baked Pears Elegante

(Serves two)

Ingredients
    2 medium, fresh pears
    3 whole cloves
    ½ cup port wine
    dash salt
    ¼ cup sugar
    3 thin lemon slices
    1 (½ -inch) stick cinnamon
    Red food coloring

Directions
Pare, halve, and core pears; place in 1 quart baking dish.

Combine all other ingredients plus a few drops red food coloring in saucepan. Bring to a boil.

Pour over pears. Bake covered at 350 F for 20 minutes.

Uncover and bake 10 minutes more.

Serve warm, topped with whipped cream.

Broccoli Casserole

Ingredients

    16 ounces frozen broccoli flowerets, thawed

    2 eggs, beaten

    1 small onion, chopped

    1 can cream of mushroom soup

    ½ cup mayonnaise

    1 cup cheddar cheese, grated (I use no-fat).

Topping

    Mix ¼ cup melted butter with ½ package of herb stuffing mix. (I skip the topping.)

Directions

Drain thawed broccoli.

Combine all ingredients in 1 ½ quart baking dish. Bake 40 minutes at 350 F or until bubbly.

This is another great recipe for a large crowd. Just double or triple the ingredients.

Chicken Salad

Ingredients
    2 cups diced, cooked chicken breasts (Cook chicken breasts in chicken stock or water with bay leaf, celery, onion, clove, salt).
    1 cups diced pineapple
    ½—3/4 cup diced celery
    ½ cup chopped walnuts

Dressing
    ½ cup sour cream
    ½ cup mayonnaise
    1/8 teaspoon salt
    ½ teaspoons Accent
    2 teaspoons lemon juice
    ½ teaspoon sugar

Directions
Combine all ingredients except nuts and refrigerate for one hour.

Place your choice of salad greens on individual plates.

Top with chicken salad. Add nuts before serving.

It goes well with lemon bread.

Cranberry Salad

Ingredients
>   2 cups water
>   1 cup sugar
>   1 pound fresh cranberries
>   1 large package lemon Jello
>   1 cup chopped walnuts
>   1 ½ cups crushed pineapple, drained

Directions
Boil sugar and water for 5 minutes.

Add cranberries.
Boil until berries pop.

Add Jello. Stir well.

Stir in pineapple and nuts.

Pour into a large glass bowl.
Allow to cool before covering with plastic wrap.

Store in refrigerator overnight.

For individual servings, pour Jello mixture into small molds. Garnish with a dollop of whipped cream, sour cream, or whipped cream cheese.

Rose Porter

Musli

Ingredients
  1 cup blanched almonds, sliced or slivered
  1 cup sunflower seeds
  3 cups rolled oats
  3/4 cup wheat germ
  3/4 cup brown sugar, packed
  ½ cup coconut
  ½ cup chocolate bits
  1 cup dried fruit, your choice, chopped into small pieces

Directions
Brown almonds and sunflower seeds at 350 F for about 10 minutes.

Cool completely.

Mix all ingredients in a large bowl.

Then store in tightly covered container in cupboard until needed.

Unbreaded Chicken Cordon Bleu

Ingredients
    4 skinless, boneless chicken breasts
    4 slices ham, thinly sliced
    4 slices Swiss cheese
    Salt and pepper
    paprika
    1 cup sliced mushrooms
    ½ cup slivered almonds

Sauce
    1 cup sour cream, diluted with sherry, white wine, or brandy until pouring consistency.

Directions
Flatten breasts with meat mallet until thin.

Season with a little salt, pepper, and paprika on both sides.

Stack ham and cheese on top of breast.

Roll up jelly-roll fashion and fasten with toothpicks.

Place in baking dish.

Cover with one cup fresh, sliced mushrooms and ½ cup slivered almonds.

Pour sauce on top and cover.
Bake at 350 F for 45 to 55 minutes. If cheese starts to run, it's done.

Rose Porter

✦ CHAPTER 15 ✦

Year Four 1976–1977
Time To Move To Another Country

DURING MY FOURTH YEAR IN GRAFENWOEHR, I STARTED ASKING FOR A TRANSFER TO Nuremberg, the nearest big city. It had a big *bahnhof* and an airport. What more could a girl want? No transfer came. I finally drove in to see the superintendent and told him I'd pay to move myself. He laughed and replied, "The American government does not accept charity, and *that* would be accepting charity." What a statement! There are some memories that you just never forget—no matter your age! About ten years later, the American government started accepting charity. A good friend and her husband moved themselves from Ramstein to Italy. But that's a later chapter.

A group of us piled into three big cars and drove to Lake Chiemsee for spring break. We rented one of Hitler's sailboats and sailed for a couple of days. The most memorable activity was taking the ferry from the military hotel across the lake to the island. For a small sum you could enter the castle to hear a concert. The castle had no furniture but lots and lots of chandeliers! You could walk around during the concert to look at the many different chandeliers, or you could sit on the floor, lean up against a pillar, and listen to the beautiful music. Later my husband and I revisited the area, but the castle was closed and concerts were no longer being held. What a shame!

Our travels north always brought us back through Cologne for lunch at McDonald's. It's across the street from the Koln Cathedral and the *bahnhof*. We never toured the cathedral or the city. We stopped only for McDonald's food! Homesick tourists always seem to end up at McDonald's. Burger King hadn't hit the European scene yet.

October always took us in the direction of Munich and the Oktoberfest, with side trips to Garmisch or Dachau. The Glockenspiel is worth a visit every trip you make. Once you've seen the Oktoberfest opening parade, the only reason to go back is for the beer tents and the chicken dance. The last time we decided it had gotten just too big, too crowded, and much too rowdy to really be a fun outing. The zoo became our favorite stop; if you ever get a chance, go with or without kids. Shopping is good also in the neighborhood of the Glockenspiel.

Nowadays, take your VAT (value added tax) forms with you and a credit or debit card. In the 70s and 80s you only got a VAT form if you took your paperwork to the VAT office. Because you had to take a number and wait for hours for your number to be called, you only did it for big purchases. You'd go through the ordeal if you were buying a new car or furniture or for extensive car repairs. Nowadays you're allowed to purchase ten VAT forms. The VAT forms cost five dollars each, so you gauge your use of them according to how much more than five dollars your items cost. We are currently using them even for manicures, pedicures, massages, and haircuts. There's been progress since the '70s! VAT tax is currently nineteen per cent so using VAT forms is a big savings for the military and civilian community.

My wonderful boss left us that spring to open a brand-new middle school in Heidelberg. A new person, not so wonderful, took over. All my friends started to PCS. The new chaplain left. The married teachers started packing out with their army husbands. My young officer friends started moving back to the States. I was tired of saying good-bye to people I loved. It's one of the negative aspects of being a DoDDS teacher.

I began to yearn for a new position in another geographical area. I applied for a transfer. Desperation makes people take desperate measures. I asked to go anywhere, which was the kiss of death! I was a slow learner, but no transfer came. I resigned. Two weeks later my transfer came through. I reminded my not-so-wonderful boss that I'd resigned. She called Nuremberg, and guess what? They couldn't find my resignation, so off I went to Taegu, Korea, kicking myself the whole way. I didn't want to leave Europe.

CHAPTER 16
1977–1978
Taegu, Korea

I left Germany with only one goal. I needed another year in an undesirable location so that I could return to a larger community in Europe. I packed my suitcase and flew from Seattle to Seoul, with a layover in Tokyo. Lots of military personnel were heading to Seoul with me. We all sat together, played backgammon, and chatted about our new adventure. When we landed in Seoul, we had to go through Customs. My passport was checked; I had no visa for Korea. Visa? What visa? DoDDS had never told me to get a visa! There I was, hours from home, with no visa. My new military buddies waved good-bye to me as they left to get on the bus for Yongsan.

After much discussion and a few phone calls, the Korean officials decided to let me into the country temporarily. I wasn't sure what was happening. I was put into a Korean military car and driven to the Yongsan army post. I was deposited at the schools' administration office. After I explained my predicament to the business manager, I was immediately rushed to the bus station and put on the bus to Taegu.

I got the last seat on the last bus bound for Taegu that afternoon, which put me in the back bench seat with the Koreans returning to Taegu after visiting relatives or shopping. I got an up-close-and-personal introduction to life in South Korea. Some women were dressed in their native dresses; some were in long skirts, and some were in mismatched outfits. It was my first introduction to *kimchi*, though I had no idea what I was smelling! The inside of the bus carried their luggage that wouldn't fit below: chickens, *yo* (a large folding bed), and assorted children, from babies to teenagers. The American girl with the "round" eyes was the main attraction for the Koreans. It was quite the ride and lasted for more than five hours. The scenery out the dirty window was gorgeous. Terraces for planting rice dotted the landscape all the way. It was August, hot and sunny. Korea was not going to be dull! And it was only for nine months.

I was met at the bus station by the high school principal. She checked me into my BOQ (Bachelor Officers Quarters) room, (Teachers were civilians with a high enough pay grade to be considered on the same pay level as the young officers. Plus we also had college degrees.) took me for dinner in the BOQ's snack bar, and introduced me to the teachers and military guys living in the building. I was told my visa would be forthcoming. I had finally arrived and would soon be legal.

No one bothered to tell me the Pacific schools start the year earlier than the German schools and that I was reporting later than what was considered kosher. They must have been saving that job for my real boss, the assistant principal. When I arrived at school the next morning, I was not disappointed. Once we got over that hurdle, we became good friends until he transferred out at the end of September.

I was shown my kindergarten classroom so that I could start setting up for my thirty morning students and thirty afternoon students. The kids who spoke English came after lunch; my morning was spent with five-year-olds who spoke no English. I was an English-as-a-second-language (ESL) teacher before ESL was a subject. What a challenge! The Korean morning kids lived with their Korean mothers and their American military fathers; there was no discipline as we know it at home.

Back in those days, kindergarten classes got no specials and no library time. The teachers had them for the entire 2 1/2-hour session with no aides. The first month of school is always hard on the students and the teacher, no matter where the school is located. The first month in Taegu was pure hell, but only the morning class. The students eventually settled into a routine that did not include hitting and biting each other when mad. Five year olds tend to get mad if someone takes a toy or book away from them. They tend to hit and ask questions later after the teacher gets involved. Behavior calms down after several phone calls home or a parent conference to alert the parents. Biting was an everyday occurrence in my morning class; biting was accepted at home with their neighborhood friends so it carried through to the American school. The afternoon class, which contained the on-post children, was pretty normal; the routines were in place early, and students were actively learning. I can't imagine being an inexperienced kindergarten teacher in Korea.

I spent my days working with the kids. In the evenings, I tried to keep busy—learning Korean, mahjong, or playing cards at someone's house or BOQ room. Manicures and pedicures were available on post or off. I had my first facial outside the Taegu gate during the winter, which was extremely cold. The girls, all three or four of them, wrapped me up in blankets to keep me warm, but the highlight was that grated carrots or cucumbers were the key ingredients for the facial. I haven't had a vegetable facial since Taegu. Massages were the same; three or four girls working on me, a stack of quilts on top to keep me warm. I must have been traumatized; after I left Taegu, I didn't get facials or massages again until twenty-plus years later!

I was anemic before I arrived in Taegu. My Florida doctor had told me to get a blood test every two or three months to monitor it. After school I'd take a taxi downtown to the Presbyterian hospital for tests. It didn't matter which afternoon I went; as soon as I walked into the waiting room, one of the Koreans, who had been waiting in line for hours to see a doctor, would take me by the arm and lead me to the front of the line. It was amazing, and I wasn't even blonde, just a round-eye. The South Koreans loved us, so the Americans got preferential treatment.

Blondes are admired by all Koreans, young and old alike. One of our new, young teachers was blonde, with matching hair on her arms. She couldn't go downtown without Korean girls and women running their hands up and down her arms. She wasn't upset by it at first, but it did get old after a few months. She'd wear long sleeves long after the ice and snow changed to warm, sunny weather.

The food stalls in the market were colorful and aromatic, filled with items you'd never wish to see in an American supermarket. Unusual body parts from cows, bulls, and pigs were on sale. Fish and other sea creatures were for sale, along with seaweed items. Fresh fruit and vegetables were plentiful. Taking pictures was always required when we visited, just so our friends at home would believe our stories. We used to buy a little pancake for a snack. The ladies would make them while we waited. It had honey and cinnamon in the center and came wrapped in an old piece of newspaper. It was delicious if you could ignore the wrapping and the sometimes odious smells of your surroundings.

Another great food item was *yaki mandu*, which are little dumplings served with a special sauce. There was a little shack right outside the back gate that delivered them to school. They were awesome! I've included the recipe; you can order the plastic mold for shaping them off the Internet or shape them yourself.

Bulgogi is a meat dish served over rice. It's yummy. *Kimchi* is fermented cabbage with lots of garlic and hot peppers. You can buy it mild, hot, or too hot to eat. Kimchi is available in the supermarkets in America. I don't plan on ever making it, so that recipe is not included. The Koreans had special clay pots in which to ferment the cabbage. They were stored on the flat roof of the houses. Everywhere, no matter what town, village, or city you traveled to, we'd see kimchi pots. There were summer recipes, winter recipes, and so forth. Check the Internet for specific ingredients.

I had my own personal sewing lady; she came every Saturday morning and made whatever item I wanted. I borrowed another teacher's sewing machine for her to use. The fabric from the market was okay, but the sewing lady requested the thread from the base exchange (BX). She seemed to think American thread was stronger than the Korean. I'm sure we were importing our thread from Korea or China, but maybe not. Maybe it was made in the USA back in those days!

On our first Saturday together, she measured me for dresses, blouses, and slacks. Then she transferred those measurements to paper and used the paper as her pattern. I've always wanted to learn how she managed it. Before I met her and after I left Korea, I sewed my own clothes. If I tore out a picture of a dress from a magazine, she'd tell me how many yards of material to buy. The following Saturday, she'd cut it out and totally finish it, right down to the buttons and hem. I never had to try on anything for her. She was the Korean Wonder Woman of seamstresses in the Taegu area. I really missed her, especially when I tried to make bound buttonholes back in the States. She charged a flat charge, no matter what she ended up sewing that Saturday. I provided her lunch, which was usually something Korean. She never asked for American food. I don't remember how much her day rate was, but it was definitely cheap and definitely worth it.

Korea is a great base for traveling in the Orient. The Korean travel office on base put together some great trips with cheap prices. The single teachers spent the holidays flying to Bangkok, Singapore, Hong Kong, Bali, Kuala Lumpur, Malaysia, Japan, Taiwan, and Okinawa.

During the two-week Christmas break, we'd visit three or four cities that had lots of tourist sites and good shopping. In Singapore we rode a rickshaw to the Raffles Hotel, the birthplace of Ernest Hemingway's Singapore Sling. We shopped in the Chinese Market, the Indian Market, and every other shopping area we could find in the two or three days allotted to Singapore. We ate in the markets during my single days. We loved the food and the bargains.

In Bangkok we visited the Oriental Hotel and saw the corridors named for famous writers who had gone to Bangkok to write, like the Ernest Hemingway and the Somerset Maugham rooms. The Oriental had everything you could possibly want: delicious food, a great location to watch the sunsets over the Chao Phraya River and its water canals, and lots of local color. You could catch a water boat on the canal to see the floating market with some boats selling bananas and other boats selling everything imaginable in the way of vegetables, fruit, and flowers.

Hong Kong had the grand old Peninsular Hotel, designed and furnished in British style. We used to go for high tea in the afternoons after walking and shopping around all day; we'd collapse in the plush overstuffed chairs and people-watch. Little boys dressed in the Peninsular Hotel uniform would walk around ringing bells, announcing a phone call for someone attending the high tea affair. Once, one of the girls went to a public phone in one of the hallways and called the Peninsular, asking for me. It was quite a thrill to hear my name being announced!

Shopping in Hong Kong meant Chinese rugs and Chinese dishes. I bought a set of a-thousand-flower dinnerware, which I later sold to another teacher. I'm glad I got rid of it because we later learned the dishes contained lead. Cherry-wood furniture was a good buy for some married couples. Teak was a favorite for party people; the monkey pod bowls from the Philippines cracked, but teak didn't. Chinese masks were great souvenirs for teaching the kids about the Chinese New Year.

China was too difficult to get to, which made it very expensive. It was about thirty minutes away as the crow flies, but travelers had to first fly to either Tokyo or Taiwan in order to then fly into and tour that great country. We had to settle for the Gobi Desert dust that would blow across during the winter months. Breathing was hard; the Koreans wore masks. Australia and New Zealand were too expensive because of the distance involved.

Antiques were a great buy. If they didn't have what you wanted, they'd tell you to come back next week and they'd have it then. The builder would find some old wood and make whatever you'd ordered, complete with brass handles and decorations. Rice measures were unique and made great magazine or knitting containers. The bridal hatboxes were great storage or end tables. The apothecary cabinets were great conversation pieces or end tables. The *tansu* was my favorite item to buy; I had three when we left Korea. A tansu provides storage for clothing; mine were trimmed in brass, with butterflies adorning the doors. All included a brass lock, which was opened by pushing another piece of brass through the lock. You ended up with a three-piece lock that all fit together. Mine featured three individual wooden pieces stacked together to make a tall cabinet; they were said to be left over from the Japanese occupation. The Japanese used them for kimonos and other clothing.

We spent the weekends traveling around Korea. Terrific Host Nation teachers helped us soak up the culture. A couple of the old-timers, teachers who had lived in Korea for years, set up trips and visits to cultural activities for those interested. Being stationed in Korea made for a close-knit group of people; you have to be close in order to survive the culture shock.

❧ CHAPTER 17 ❧
1978–1979
Tampa, Florida

AFTER MY NINE MONTHS WERE UP, I TOOK A YEAR OFF. I SPENT A YEAR IN TAMPA, teaching at an upper-middle-class elementary school. That was culture shock after Korea. The big item in the stores that June was the plastic lettuce twirler; we still have them. You put wet lettuce leaves inside the slotted bowl, press the lid on, turn the handle, and the water twirls off your lettuce leaves, drying them for a stupendous green salad. I almost fainted when I saw it for the first time. Korea had made a big impression on me, and I hadn't even realized it until I got back home. We were spending three dollars on a plastic container, when a Korean family could eat for a week on three dollars.

I had not gone home to teach. I had no letters of recommendation with me, nothing to impress a principal. I had gone home to get certified to teach middle-school math. Due to family circumstances, however, I went looking for a job. I interviewed for one of the two openings in the entire county. The principal listened to me talk about DoDDS in general and Korea in particular and hired me on the spot. When I left in June to go back to Korea, he was as surprised as I was. I'd wanted to return to Europe, but the rules said I needed an official transfer. I had only been approved for a year's leave of absence.

Years later when Frank and I returned to Tampa, my principal had finished his PhD and was the director of human resources. I called one of my old teacher friends from that school and learned she had become a principal. I got rehired at the same upper-middle-class elementary school as before. You can't burn your bridges when you leave a school. It's often who you know who gets you the job or the transfer.

⟡ CHAPTER 18 ⟡
1979–1982
Seoul, Korea

I RETURNED TO KOREA BUT NOT TO THE SMALL CITY OF TAEGU. INSTEAD I MOVED to the big city of Seoul. I arrived with a visa already in my passport, and I was on time for the start of the school year. The union was alive and well by that time. I got off the military plane at Osan Air Force Base and heard one of the returning teachers ask a union representative if a certain assistant principal had died yet? I was appalled, wondering what had I gotten myself into. I'd never heard another teacher voice such contempt for an evaluator. You have to remember that two of my three previous principals had walked on water.

Before my two years in a combined grades two and three class ended, I found myself remembering my arrival at Osan and that teacher's question many times. The assistant principal was single; an alcoholic who we swear drank on the job. He adopted three Korean children and then went home one summer through Hawaii and dumped the kids there in foster care. The oldest girl wrote back to our principal, and tales were told. He had been a totally worthless individual with his adopted children too. As the rumor goes, he was never heard from again. He's probably my very worst story about life at the military schools.

Nevertheless, I loved Seoul: lots of people, very bad traffic with really awful drivers, lots of good shopping, and good restaurants. A favorite night out for the teachers was to go to the Demilitarized Zone (DMZ) for an all-night party. First, we took the military tour of the DMZ area, complete with barbed wire and no man's land. Then came the party at the local military drinking hole. Once eleven o'clock came, everyone was destined to spend the rest of the night there, drinking, dancing, and talking to the guys. When five in the morning came, the teachers were ready to drive back to Yongsan and get some much-needed sleep. It was something to do once, but once was enough for me.

Another way to prevent boredom was to take flying lessons. I'd drive to Osan, about an hour away, and meet my instructor for an hour's lesson. I gave up the lessons early on when I discovered I got airsick every time I went up. Another problem was trying to figure out what the Korean air traffic controller was saying. I wasn't a seasoned pilot with an idea of what I should be hearing, and deciphering the poorly pronounced English in a Korean accent was too much for me to handle.

After two years in a 2-3 combination class, I applied for a transfer and got an assignment back to Germany. I was in heaven. I was even willing to give up my new sewing lady, Mrs. Hur, to return. Mrs. Hur was a real businesswoman. She came to school one afternoon each week; all the teachers would take turns talking to her, showing her magazine or catalog pictures of three-piece suits, blouses, dresses, or slacks. We'd pick out material from the samples she'd bring. If you had ordered an item the previous week, you'd have to try it on and let her make adjustments the following week. She wasn't cheap, but she was reasonable. Your finished item took three weeks, but who cared? We had lined wool three-piece suits with bound buttonholes for about one-fifth what they'd cost in the States.

I had my orders in my hand, my pack-out date, and my airplane reservations. And then I met Frank one Friday night at the Embassy Club. Several of us were sitting with the superintendent and his wife during happy hour. Frank came over and introduced himself; my girlfriend, sitting next to me muttered under her breath, "Get rid of him!" Three weeks later I found myself in the superintendent's office, asking if I could turn down the transfer. He approved the paperwork, and I stayed another year. I moved to a 4-5 class with a different assistant principal.

My classroom was half of a Quonset hut with a storeroom in the middle of it. I could see the left half of my kids or the right half of my kids, a total of thirty-five. If I stood in front of the chalkboard, I could see all thirty-five at the same time. Yes, thirty-five were a lot, but the teachers had voted to use two teacher slots as science specialists. Our students took science twice a week from science specialists, and those kids learned a lot of science. They worked hands on and produced great science scores on the annual achievement tests. About three months into the year, I asked the AP (assistant principal) if the storeroom could be torn out. He said of course. No one had ever complained about it before. It didn't store anything besides his bike, which could be parked safely in his office.

Koreans like Americans. And American teachers loved the Korean children and their parents. There's nothing like teaching Oriental children and being treated with the respect teachers deserve. I've never changed my feelings about Orientals as students; I love them. It doesn't matter where in the world those kids are being taught, they are the teacher's favorites.

Etae Won was the shopping mecca of Seoul for the American military community. We'd walk out the Yongsan gate, turn right, and walk for ten minutes to where we'd shop till we dropped. You could go dancing, drinking, or shopping in Etae Won. Silk shirts were made to order in less than a week, as were running suits, tailor-made suits, shoes, lamps, anything. The beer was made from a formaldehyde mix, or at least that was the joke everyone told. We were often found on Friday nights in our favorite disco. We'd walk up to dance and everybody else would sit down. I never understood that ritual. We definitely were not Fred Astaire and Ginger Rogers, but we were the only round eyes in the establishment! There was a curfew, which meant you had to be back inside the Yongsan gate by eleven at night or you stayed inside until five in the morning. No one was allowed on the Korean streets during the curfew.

Before getting married, Frank had to complete a military questionnaire about me. He had to include a list of all the countries I'd traveled to during my time overseas. His comment at the time was that the military would not allow *him* to visit half the countries I'd been to because of his security clearance. When he'd graduated from tech school, the KGB had supposedly sent his class a congratulatory telegram; it was their way of putting them on notice! Someone representing Uncle Sam was also sent to my old neighborhood to ask questions. I must have passed the inspection! But they continued to check Frank out every two years.

Getting married in Korea is too frustrating; too many friends had tried it and had made three trips before all the paperwork was completed. Besides, I was marrying an American, so five months later we flew to Hawaii to get married.

Mrs. Hur made my wedding dress. She didn't like the local lace. I had picked out a dress from a magazine, and she calculated the amount of lace I needed to buy during my summer trip to Florida. She chose a silk to go with the lace, and my dress was finished with Korean love and workmanship. It was a two-piece outfit; both pieces together made the wedding dress. Without the lace it was a just a party dress. I wore it to my twenty-year class reunion the following summer. I haven't worn the slip dress lately, but it is packed away, waiting for the appropriate event.

Frank was on assignment, so we decided to meet in Hawaii to get married. We picked the Hilton Royal Hawaiian Village over the military's Hale Koa, because, at that time, the Hilton was cheaper. It isn't anymore. Since I was the lucky one, I landed in Honolulu first. I tried to check into our room at the Hawaiian Hilton in Waikiki. No way would the Hilton let me check into Frank's room; that was not allowed! I had to check into my own room. Frank was flying in later, and when he arrived that night, guess whose room the Hilton gave him a key to? I was beyond ticked! We went ahead and made arrangements for the Hilton photographer; we reserved the Fort Derussy Chapel and asked a chaplain to perform the ceremony.

The big day came; we all met at the chapel door. The chaplain had driven over with three sets of keys. He arrived by himself, so we needed another witness. While Chaplain Carter tried to open the door, Frank walked over to the Class 6, our liquor store, and asked them to call the MPs; someone was trying to break into the chapel! By the time the military police arrived, Chaplain Carter had tried every one of the keys on the three key rings. None of them worked! We went ahead and signed the paperwork, and the MP and the photographer acted as our two witnesses. The question was, did we still want the ceremony since we couldn't get into the church? Of course, we did! Our vows were exchanged outside the chapel under the trees with the sweet smelling flowers. We were legally married.

We've been back twice to renew our vows, but we've gotten smarter. Now we go back on a Sunday for morning services when the chapel is open. Our renewal service has been performed afterward.

We bought our first miniature schnauzer, Snoozer, while living in Seoul. He was a male and barked a lot if someone rang the doorbell. The Koreans were scared to death of dogs. Our Snoozer just wanted to play. If a Korean came to our apartment door, he would not come inside until we had picked up the barking dog or put him out on the balcony. One day I was home with a sprained ankle, and Snoozer saw some kids playing in the courtyard. He wanted to play, too, so he jumped off our fifth-floor balcony, landed in a shrub, and ran off to play with the kids. I didn't miss him right away, but when I did, I panicked and called Frank at work. I could see him running around with the kids, but I couldn't get to him in a very rapid fashion. Eventually, Frank made it home, but I had already climbed down the five floors with my crutches and walked over to him. No way was he going to leave the fun and follow me home until Frank arrived like the White Knight. Then Snoozer was happy to go home. The first time we took him to be groomed was traumatizing for me. He was delivered back to us looking just like the pictures of schnauzers in our dog books—not like our cuddly little ball of fur! I couldn't even look at him without being upset. My cute ball of fluff was gone forever.

The best story I have from Seoul is seeing the TR-1 take off. I was never told when the planes were landing or taking off at Osan Air Force Base. It was always a big secret. One Friday night Frank said we had to be at Osan Air Base at about seven the next morning. I refused. No way was I getting up at five on a Saturday after five long days of teaching just to drive for an hour to Osan. Eventually I got the unspoken message. If I ever wanted to see a TR-1 take off, I'd better be at Osan at seven. We were there, and it was a glorious sight. I've never seen anything to compare with it, not even the space shuttles taking off at Cape Canaveral.

Another humorous story involved an artist who was considered a national treasure by the Koreans. We had gone to a party at the house of a teacher who had been in Korea for fifteen years. The teacher knew lots of Koreans and spoke Korean. One of his friends was a painter. He had painted a winter tiger for our friend, who hung it in his living room. We fell in love with it and wanted one too. The painter agreed to do one for us, but he painted a summer tiger. The story of the tiger was painted on the left side and officially signed. We couldn't read it, of course, so we assumed it was just a normal story with signature. It was given to us rolled up like a poster. We paid the national-treasure artist the price he asked and immediately took it to a reputable framer.

The framer took one look at it and understood the true value of it. We knew the painter was famous, but we didn't fully understand how famous. The framer immediately asked us where we had gotten it. Frank told him it had been a gift; if you're given a gift, a Korean will not steal it. It's against their values. When we returned to pick up our framed painting, it was hanging in a special place of honor, waiting for us. We pack it up and take it with us in a special wooden box each time we changed duty stations.

That painter later attended a party on post. Lots of female teachers attended the party. In Korea it's quite common for the men to leave their wives at home while they party with the local girls. The painter looked around at all the single female teachers and asked which ones were the special girls. We never told the teachers about his question.

On another occasion Frank took me to a party with the Koreans from his office. We arrived at the restaurant's special room where the party was to be held. As soon as we walked in, we knew something was not quite right. I was the only female. We had a delightful dinner with six high-ranking Koreans and left. After we left, I guess the girls got their dinner! The Koreans had assumed Frank knew it was for men only, no wives, but he was a newlywed.

The best field trip we took that year was one Frank set up for my grades four and five combination class. We drove from one base to another so that the kids could have hands-on experience with several of the military's flying machines. The students were excited to actually sit inside a helicopter. Our only problem was getting back in time for the buses; we didn't, but parents weren't upset when they learned why.

The funniest story is that people like us who loved Mexican food had to drive all the way to Osan to get some. If the on-base restaurant ran out of ingredients, which was all the time, you got strange substitutions; ketchup for tomato sauce, mozzarella for cheddar, Tabasco for taco sauce.

As in any other large city, Seoul had "ladies of the night." Along the Etae Won strip were several bars with ladies working close by. In case you're in the area after dark, look for a curtain pulled across a large lit window. There's always a brass candlestick, which has an intricately cut butterfly attached to it that is lit after dark. If the saleslady is free, you'll see the light from a candle. If she's busy with a customer, she moves the butterfly in front of the flame. If you need a great conversation piece and souvenir of Korea, these candelabras can be bought in any brass store.

The most serious incident that ever happened occurred the night of our last Christmas party in Seoul. It was held on December 12 at one of the special clubs. All the teachers, husbands, administrators, and boyfriends attended the Christmas gathering. A great time was had by all. Sometime during the festivities an announcement was made that the current leader of South Korea had been murdered in a coup d'etat. His predecessor, dictator and president Park Chung-hee, had been assassinated in 1979. We went home for the night, wondering what this meant for the students and dependents.

The next day we discovered that the party-goers who lived across the Hahn River Bridge had spent the night on the bridge because no one was allowed to leave the city. It was one of the times we were sure we would be evacuated. We had always lived with the notion of an evacuation at the back of our minds; I never let my car's gas tank get below half full, just in case we had to head for Pusan. We always had coffee, Corning Ware, bananas, or Scotch available to bribe our way down south to the port.

My worst tale of woe involved another wonderful Toyota. I had shipped my brand-new, fire-engine-red Toyota Celica with me to Seoul. It was hit three times in three years, twice while it was stationary in a parking lot. The first time, we had driven to a town in the south to check out some burial tombs. We spent the night at a hotel. Around three in the morning we were awakened by the hotel night manager. It seems my car had been broadsided by a taxi driver who'd fallen asleep at the wheel. Working with the Korean police and filling out reports and insurance claims was definitely a bad experience. I don't recommend being in an accident in Korea.

The second time Frank was driving it to Seoul University, where we were both teaching English. We were in a four-car bang-up in traffic. Those happen a lot. Korean drivers are insane. They make four lanes out of two painted lanes or ten lanes out of six.

The third time it was sitting in a parking lot on Yongsan Air Base. A US mail truck backed into it! It turned out to be *my fault* because I was not legally registered to have it. Frank and I had just gotten married. The military police assumed I was his dependent wife; families were only authorized one car. It was a man's world, so Frank was the lucky person who could own a car. It took a few phone conversations, but since I was self-sponsored, I got to keep my banged-up, brand-new, fire-engine-red Toyota Celica registered! I'm firmly convinced it was hit because it was red. The moral of the story is don't buy a red car. I haven't owned one since.

One of our trips to see burial mounds involved staying for lunch at the gift shop and restaurant. The menu was so funny that I talked the manager into letting me take one as a souvenir. It's still on our bookcase in a special place. On the menu were dried "titbits," otherwise known as tidbits, but no description was printed on the menu.

During my first two years in Korea, I never ate in tourist restaurants or tourist hotels. The food in these restaurants was considered safe for Americans to eat. Special care was taken when preparing the food to meet our hygienic standards. When I started dating Frank, he refused to eat in the local places I liked. I had to switch over to the "safe" restaurants. I had never gotten sick from the Korean food I'd eaten for two years in the local restaurants. Suddenly, in my third year in Korea, I was sick many times from eating in the safe restaurants. Later, when we PCSed to Ramstein, my stomach problems cleared up. I don't know what the moral of that story is. I guess my Korean flora didn't like my tourist hotel flora!

The following spring, I applied for a transfer and got orders to Ramstein Elementary School. When Frank's orders arrived for Ramstein, his general told him he had bad news and good news. The good news was he had his transfer to Ramstein Air Force Base. The bad news was that the headquarters building had just been blown up. That was the beginning of long lines at the gates, mirrors checking under the cars, and barricades.

Frank wanted to stay in Korea; he had a great job tasking the SR-71 and the TR-1. Frank's general asked me to stay another year. I laughed. Frank could stay in Korea, but I was returning to Germany. We moved to Ramstein Air Force Base.

Here are some of my favorite recipes from my four years in Korea. We had many parties, and we ate very well!

Coconut Pie

Ingredients
    4 eggs
    ½ stick butter, melted
    2 cups milk
    1 cup coconut
    ¼ teaspoon salt
    1 teaspoon vanilla
    ½ teaspoon baking powder
    1 cup sugar
    ½ cup flour

Directions
Combine ingredients in a large bowl.

Mix until smooth.

Pour into greased 10-inch pie pan.

Bake at 350 F for 1 hour and 5 minutes.

Refrigerate leftovers.

Rose Porter

Corn Casserole

Ingredients
  2 (16-ounce) cans cream corn
  1 can regular corn, drained
  12 ounces Swiss cheese, grated
  3 eggs, beaten
  1 can sweetened condensed milk
  1 ½ packages saltine crackers, crushed*

Directions
Grease a 2-quart casserole dish.

Mix all ingredients and pour into casserole dish.

Bake at 350 F for 40 minutes or until top is brown.

*If you don't have a rolling pin, put the saltines in a plastic Ziploc. Use a can of veggies as your rolling pin.

Glazed Fruit Compote

Serves 4

Ingredients
  2 medium oranges
  ¼ cup light brown sugar, packed
  4 tablespoons butter
  ¼ teaspoon cinnamon
  4 large bananas
  1 jigger Amaretto

Directions
Grate 2 tablespoons orange peel from oranges. Set aside.

Peel oranges and slice into ½ -inch slices. All of the white outer layer should be cut away.

Over low heat, heat brown sugar, butter, and cinnamon until mixture is melted and begins to boil, stirring frequently.

Cut bananas into 2-inch chunks. Blend bananas and oranges into butter mixture and heat thoroughly, gently turning fruit.

Sprinkle with orange peel. Stir in one jigger Amaretto.

Serve immediately.

Great Corn Bread

Ingredients
    1-2/3 cups flour
    2/3 cup sugar
    5 teaspoons baking powder
    1 teaspoon salt
    1-2/3 cup cornmeal
    2 eggs, separated
    1-2/3 cups milk
    1 cup butter, melted

Directions
Sift flour, sugar, baking powder, and salt into a large bowl.

Stir in cornmeal until well blended.

Beat egg yolks until thick. Combine with milk and stir into dry ingredients to make a smooth batter.

Stir in melted butter until blended. Do not over-stir.

Fold in stiffly beaten egg whites.

Pour into well-greased 9-inch loaf pan.

Bake at 425 F for 40 minutes.

Cool for 10 minutes. Serve with butter and honey.

Cooked Playdough

(For the classroom)

Ingredients
  1-1/2 cups flour
  3/4 cup salt
  1-1/2 tablespoons oil
  1 tablespoon cream of tartar
  1-1/2 cups water
  Food coloring

Directions
Mix all ingredients thoroughly. It will look like pancake mix.

In a three quart pot cook over medium heat, stirring constantly.

Let cool and knead until pliable.

Rose Porter

Hot Wings

Ingredients
  2-1/2 pounds chicken wings, disjointed
  1 (8-ounce) bottle hot sauce
  1 stick butter
  1 tablespoon Tabasco sauce
  1 teaspoon garlic powder
  1 teaspoon paprika
  One dash salt

Directions
Bake wings in 375 F oven for 35 minutes. Turn over and bake another 30 minutes, or until golden brown. Drain on paper towels.

Melt butter in saucepan and add the rest of the ingredients. Bring to a boil; simmer for 20 minutes.

Add chicken wings to sauce, making sure all are covered. They can be served immediately or allowed to simmer in the sauce for another 30 minutes.

Serve 6 wings at a time with cold salads and ranch dressing. Any of these would be great: Cole slaw, a tossed salad with ranch dressing, a macaroni salad, fruit salad, or celery and carrot sticks.

Keep the remainder of the wings on the stove on very low heat.

Recipe is easily adapted for a large party. Sauce can be frozen.

Italian Creme Cake

Ingredients

    1 stick butter, softened
    ½ cup shortening
    2 cups sugar
    5 eggs, separated
    2 cups flour
    1 cup buttermilk*
    1 teaspoon soda
    ½ teaspoon salt
    1 cup coconut
    1 cup chopped walnuts
    1 teaspoon vanilla

Directions
Beat egg whites until stiff.
Cream butter, shortening, and sugar together.
Add egg yolks one at a time.
Sift flour, soda, and salt together.
Add flour mixture, alternating with buttermilk.
Add vanilla, coconut, and nuts.
Fold in egg whites.

Pour into 3 greased and floured 9-inch pans.
Bake in preheated 350 F oven for 25 minutes.

*If you don't have buttermilk, mix milk with one teaspoon cider vinegar.

Frosting

    8 ounces cream cheese
    ½ stick butter
    1 box powdered sugar
    1 teaspoon vanilla*

Cream the cream cheese and butter together until smooth.

Gradually add powdered sugar and vanilla.

Spread frosting on each layer.

Leave the sides free of frosting.

*Here's a tip for making your own vanilla: Buy a small bottle of vodka and 2 or 3 vanilla beans. Add beans to vodka bottle. Store in cabinet for 2 weeks before using.

Kentucky Derby Pie

Ingredients
    1 cup sugar
    ½ cup flour
    1 stick butter, melted and cooled
    2 eggs, beaten
    1/3 to ½ cup bourbon
    1 teaspoon vanilla
    1 (6-ounce) package chocolate chips
    1 cup walnuts, chopped
    One unbaked pie shell

Directions
Mix sugar and flour.
Add eggs and butter.
Add bourbon.
Stir in nuts, chocolate chips, and vanilla.

Pour into unbaked pie shell.

Bake at 350 F for 30 minutes.

Test by sticking a toothpick in the center. If toothpick comes out clean, it's ready. If unclean, bake for another 5 minutes and then test again.

Cool on a wire rack.

Serve warm with whipped cream or vanilla ice cream.

Korean Bulgogi

Ingredients
    1 pound sirloin
    4 tablespoons sugar
    2 tablespoons oil
    6 tablespoons soy sauce
    1 green onion, chopped
    1 clove garlic, chopped
    4 tablespoons prepared sesame seeds
    1 tablespoon flour
    Water
    Salt and pepper

Directions
Cut beef into slices. Add sugar and oil. Mix well.

Combine soy sauce, chopped onion, salt, pepper, chopped garlic, sesame seeds, and flour.

Add to meat. Let stand 15 minutes.

Fry in a small amount oil until tender. Cover slightly after it's well browned. Add a small amount of water, cover with lid, and steam until meat is tender.

Serve hot with rice.

Piña Colada Chiffon Pie

Serves 8

Ingredients

Crust
    1 cup graham cracker crumbs
    1/3 cup flaked coconut
    ¼ cup butter, melted

Filling
    1 (20-ounce) can crushed pineapple with juice
    2 envelopes unflavored gelatin
    1 (15-ounce) can cream of coconut
    2 large eggs, separated
    1/3 cup orange juice or dark rum
    1 cup heavy cream
    ¼ cup sugar

Directions
Pie crust

Combine crumbs and coconut. Stir in melted butter.
Press mixture evenly onto bottom and sides of 9-inch pie plate.
Freeze.

Filling
Drain pineapple; put juice in medium-size saucepan. Reserve crushed pineapple.
Sprinkle gelatin over juice in saucepan. Let stand 5 minutes.

Place saucepan over very low heat, stirring constantly until gelatin is dissolved, about 3 to 5 minutes.

In a stainless-steel saucepan, combine cream of coconut and egg yolks and cook over low heat for 5 minutes, stirring constantly, until mixture is very hot but not simmering. Remove from heat.

Stir melted gelatin mixture into cream of coconut mixture.
Stir in orange juice or rum and crushed pineapple.

Spoon mixture into large bowl. Cool for 15 minutes and then chill in refrigerator for at least 45 minutes, or until mixture mounds easily with spoon.

Using the same beaters, beat the heavy cream at high speed until stiff peaks form when beaters are lifted. Fold into gelatin mixture.

Using clean beaters and a clean glass bowl, beat egg whites at high speed until foamy. Add sugar, 1 tablespoon at a time. Beat until stiff peaks form when the beater is lifted. Fold egg whites into gelatin mixture. Spoon filling into crust. Refrigerate pie at least 1 hour to set.

Garnish pie with pineapple chunks and coconut, if desired.

Sweet Potato Casserole

Ingredients
    1 can (18 ounces) sweet potatoes
    ½ cup brown sugar, packed
    ½ teaspoon salt

¼ cup each:
    butter
    coconut
    chopped walnuts
    raisins
    light cream
    small marshmallows

Directions
Mash sweet potatoes in a bowl.

Melt butter in a casserole pan; add brown sugar and stir well.

Add sweet potatoes. Mix well.

Add the rest of the ingredients and mix well.

Top with small marshmallows and bake in moderate oven 350 F for 20–25 minutes, or until marshmallows melt and brown.

This casserole goes great with a beef roast, turkey, or ham.

Rose Porter

Taco Salad

Ingredients
    1 pound ground sirloin
    1 package (1 ounce) taco mix
    1 can (15 ounces) kidney beans, drained and rinsed
    1 head iceberg lettuce, torn into small pieces
    1 large onion, chopped
    3 large tomatoes, chopped
    2 cups cheddar cheese, shredded
    8 ounces French dressing
    taco chips and salsa

Directions
Fry sirloin in pan. Add taco mix and kidney beans. Continue frying until beef is no longer pink. If mixture becomes too dry, add a little water. Remove from heat and drain.

Mix lettuce, chopped onion, chopped tomatoes, and cheese together. Toss with dressing. Serve salad in large plates or pasta bowls.

Add sirloin mixture as a topping. Garnish with taco chips and salsa to taste.

Note: Chicken breasts cut into pieces can be substituted for ground sirloin.

Bags of salad greens can be substituted for the iceberg lettuce.

Yaki Mandu

This recipe was given to teachers at Seoul American Elementary School by our host-nation teacher. Every school has at least one HN teacher to teach local customs, numbers, phrases, and so forth to the children. The dough is pretty standard; the ingredients depend on you and your taste buds. We like all the ingredients, so I experiment with the amounts. You can do the same.

Dough
    3 to 4 cups flour
    1 egg
    1 tablespoon oil
    Water

Filling
    1 onion, chopped
    1 teaspoon salt
    ½ cup bean sprouts
    3 bacon slices
    8 ounces ground beef
    2 teaspoons garlic
    1 teaspoon black pepper
    ½ teaspoon red pepper flakes

Directions
To make the dough: mix all ingredients together until it is smooth. Add a little water at a time and fold into dough, until dough is soft but not gooey or sticky. Put into a bowl; cover dough with a wet cloth.

Sprinkle onion pieces with salt and let set for five minutes; squeeze out juice on a paper towel. Boil 2-3 cups water in a covered pot; cook bean sprouts lightly, about 3 minutes. Drain, run cold water over them, and squeeze out water with paper towel. Cut bacon into small pieces; cut beef into small pieces. Fry and drain. Put all ingredients into a bowl and flavor with ½ teaspoon salt and pepper, garlic, and red pepper flakes. Mix with hands.

Roll out dough in a long skinny roll. Then slice it into small, thin layers (like refrigerator cookies). Roll it out into about 18-20 round circles. Fill with some filling. Brush egg white around the edges. Fold it over, and seal the edges.

Boil water in a large pot. Put in yaki mandu and boil again for around 5 minutes. Take out of pan and fry in vegetable oil until brown.

Note:
> You can bake mandu in the oven on a greased cookie sheet.

To make water mandu, boil water in a large pasta type pot, boil mandu for around 10 minutes. Don't fry in oil.

Dipping Sauce
> ¼ cup soy sauce
> 2 teaspoons rice vinegar
> 1 teaspoon sesame oil
> 1 teaspoon red pepper flakes

Mix ingredients and you're ready to taste.

✦ CHAPTER 19 ✦

1982–1993
Ramstein Elementary School

THE HEADQUARTERS BUILDING WAS BOMBED BEFORE WE LEFT KOREA IN 1982. WE arrived at Ramstein Air Force Base in early July. After the headquarters bombing, security on all our overseas bases was heightened. For teachers, parents, and students, it meant getting up even earlier so that we could get to school on time. Just to get on base, lines for security checks took one to two hours. The buses had their own gate, which opened just for them, but getting to that gate took extra time; the drivers and students had to sit in lines too. We started eating breakfast on base just out of necessity. We'd get there about six fifteen and sit with a group of teachers, to eat and chat until seven thirty or seven forty-five. It wasn't much fun, but that was what you had to do to make it to school on time. Living in Germany was worth it!

Breakfast was served at the snack bar. You probably remember the kind I'm referring to: you followed the line down the rail with your food tray, past all the pastries, junk food, milk cartons, until you reached the cook. Then you'd order eggs, toast, pancakes, and so forth. My group used to get the biscuit. My mouth still waters when I think of that biscuit! Homemade with lard, I'm sure, probably no less than a thousand calories per biscuit. Nobody would dare order two!

When Chernobyl blew, we were eating biscuits. Twenty of our middle school students were touring Moscow and Leningrad at the time. They visited schools, stayed in youth hostels, and met with Russian students. While they were there, they were unaware of the turmoil we were feeling back in the snack bar. They returned safely, but we never knew if they had ever been in any danger.

Ramstein school's most famous story is the field trip by train to the Karlsruhe Zoo. Eight classes participated, and a great time was had by all—until the trip back to school. A man was transporting a monkey inside his jacket from a zoo in Switzerland to a zoo in Germany. Second graders on a field trip are especially curious, and more so when a monkey is sitting in the car with them. As seven-year-olds naturally will, many wanted to see the monkey up close. It got too personal for several—the monkey attacked them. I was the lucky teacher of the injured students. Thank goodness, the parents were chaperoning the trip. When the police and train officials wanted to take the children off the train to take them to a medical facility, the parents said no. They elected to stay on the train and to take their kids to the American hospital in Landstuhl.

Evidently, the police and the train officials had a pow-wow after we left the station and decided they knew what was best for the children—or at least the train's reputation. Of course, by that time, the officials were asking themselves how the man had been allowed to transport the monkey without his cage. It wasn't the children's fault they'd been attacked.

To make a long story short, halfway home the train made an unscheduled stop in Landau. Several cops and medical people boarded; ambulances were standing by to take the kids to the German hospital. Again, the parents said no.

The train arrived back in Landstuhl after six that Friday night, and parents drove their kids straight to the emergency room for treatment. None were injured seriously. One of our veterinarians told a parent that a monkey will attack anything that moves and that it should never have been transported outside a cage.

I do wish the school had gotten some information from the officials about their discussion with the zoo officials or the home office. Knowing the German government the way we did, I'm sure some official correspondence transpired between the zoo managers and the train officials.

A great trip for visitors to the area is the Rhine River Castle Cruise, which lasts from early morning to late afternoon. We took Frank's aunt and uncle and their friends on a sunny day in June; we were lucky with the weather. The relatives loved the cruise and the food. We'd all order drinks, but Frank's aunt would just order tonic. We didn't understand it—we knew she was a drinker. Before we returned home, however, we discovered her trick. She carried miniatures in her purse. After we caught her, we learned she refilled them each night from her gin bottle in the hotel. After that we just smiled until they flew back to California.

Before they left, we took them to one of our favorite restaurants in Kaiserslautern. It's called the Balkan Grill and has been run for thirty-plus years by a Yugoslavian we met in 1982. He always referred to Frank as the Capitalist, and Frank called him the Socialist. Whenever we see a Balkan Grill restaurant, we usually manage to visit while we're in the neighborhood. The food is grilled and served with unusual sides: chopped onions and a bell pepper sauce called *ajvar*, plus the usual red rice, fries, salad, string beans, or green lima beans. Their liqueur is unusual also, a mixture of plum brandy and slivovitz. You don't want the slivovitz by itself. We were served it that way once in Berlin—never again! It's potent.

Frank worked for NATO after he transferred to Ramstein. Once a month one of the British officers would host a dinner party at his apartment; they all lived in the highrises close to the army hospital in Landstuhl. The party was never on a weekend, so I always had to go on a school night; parties during the school week have never been popular with me. We'd arrive at six o'clock, drink and socialize until eight; then dinner would be served buffet style. It was always something with bread and rice: chili over rice, spaghetti sauce over rice, vegetable stew over rice, and so forth. Then there'd be more drinking until ten or ten thirty. Usually three yummy desserts would be presented then. It seems everyone really came to drink and eat dessert. After dessert, there was coffee or tea. Then we could finally go home. Never once did we get any finger food.

My husband decided we'd have them over and serve as much messy finger food as possible, forcing them to get their fingers really sticky! We served no rice and no bread. They loved their gin, so Frank made an Emerald Punch, using a recipe borrowed from his gin-loving aunt. It's another one of those potent punches. And, yes, the recipe is included, for those of you who wish to try it! We served barbecued pork ribs with sticky honey in the sauce, corn on the cob, hot wings, chips and veggies and dips, and some nonsticky salads. Desserts were regular items like chocolate layer cake, rum cake, and ice cream. The British guests loved the punch and drank it like water. The messy food was eaten with finger-licking gusto, which made Frank laugh out loud throughout the night.

Dessert was over by nine, and everyone left at nine thirty so that I could get up and face second graders the next morning. Frank had been drilling them with the information that all Americans went to bed at nine thirty. They must have believed him. Besides, there was no way I was staying awake until midnight in my own house! We never got any feedback on the dinner except that the punch was wonderful and everybody had headaches the next day. I find it hard to believe they didn't have headaches after the other parties we'd attended!

Ramstein is a great jumping off place to visit other countries. It's one hour from the Frankfurt Airport and about 30 minutes from the Saarbrucken Airport. Many countries are within driving distances and you must go to Holland to see the tulips in the spring. The Dutch never close their curtains because they feel they have nothing to hide. When the houses are lit for dinner, you can see the entire family around the table. The children eventually go to bed, but the adults sit and watch TV or read with the world outside their house watching. It's an interesting concept. Maybe that why the *"ladies of the night"* sit in lit windows reading their book until a business transaction takes them inside the house away from all the watching eyes in the alley.

❦ C H A P T E R 2 0 ❦
Our Miniature Schnauzers

WE BOUGHT A MALE MINIATURE SCHNAUZER WHILE IN KOREA AND BOUGHT MISSY, a female, in Texas. We wanted to register them with the Deutsche Kennel Club, but they didn't like our dogs. The German breed has less terrier and more Affenpinscher included in its ancestry. The American breed is too tall, and their necks are longer, due to the terrier blood lines bred into them during WWI. We went ahead and had a litter of puppies anyway. When the puppies were newborn, a German vet came to the house and docked their tails. When it was time, we had their ears clipped by a French vet in nearby Forbach, France. The kindergarten teachers wanted us to bring the puppies to school, so when the puppies were old enough Frank took them to school. That was a real treat for several classes. The teachers were still asking about the puppies two years later!

We spent our first year in Eulenbis, a village on the top of a hill about fifteen minutes from Ramstein. When we first moved into our rental house, Frank took Missy out to see the moo-cows that came up to our back fence, as well as the herds of sheep. A cow took one look at Missy and gave her a big lick with her enormous tongue. The look on Missy's face showed she was one disgusted dog! After that, all you had to say to get Missy or Snoozer to go outside was "go catch a cow." They would immediately come awake from a nap or stop eating a snack and run outside, barking as loudly as they possibly could.

When it came time to move from Eulenbis to the village at the foot of the hill, our German neighbor came by to tell us about Missy's yearlong adventures. Without our knowledge, Missy dug out from under the backyard fence every morning after we left for work, and she would run across the street to Herr Reiss' house to spend the day with them and, more importantly, their handsome Irish setter! Before we were due to arrive home in the afternoon, Herr or Frau Reiss would bring her home and put her back inside our yard! That went on for one solid year without our neighbors telling us. Missy was a real beauty and very used to getting her own way, so I guess they liked her company. They were probably afraid we'd fix the fence so that she couldn't dig out from under it.

Then we moved to a new house in the next village, closer to Ramstein. Missy and Snoozer got together again, but by this time we'd bought another female on a home visit to Texas. Missy had her litter, and Cinderella wanted to help her with the puppies. Missy wouldn't let her near the puppies.

Cinder had a body much like the German dogs so we wanted to have Cinder's paperwork registered with the German Kennel Club. In order to do that, we had to show her. We took her to a dog show and were told she could *never* have a litter registered in Germany because she had crooked teeth! Evidently, having crooked teeth makes you a bad mother! It was suggested that we do something about her teeth.

Now, what do you do about a puppy's crooked teeth? We thought the German officials were nuts. But we took her to a German vet to ask for help. We were told to take her to a "special" vet, about an hour away from Ramstein, who could put braces on her for a rather large sum of money. We wanted to register her in Germany because we were living there. To make a long story short, the vet put braces on her, charged us an arm and a leg for his expertise, took them off after the appropriate time passed, and her teeth were still crooked!

The first time Cinder went into heat, we took Snoozer, the male, to the kennel because she was too young to be a mother. We thought we had Cinder's fertile time covered by putting the male schnauzer in the kennel. Well, we failed. Snoozer came home from the kennel and promptly went for our little Cinderella! As Mother Nature had intended, she delivered five healthy puppies two months later. That was the September we missed the big once-a-year Ramstein Bazaar. We didn't want to leave our expectant mother to deliver while we were out shopping for Christmas presents! She was so young, and I was too nervous. After all, she had never been through the birthing process, and I was an experienced observer.

As strange as it sounds, when Missy tried to help Cinder with her puppies, Cinder let her. Missy produced milk and nursed the puppies too. While the puppies were growing and nursing, Frank's aunt and uncle came to visit. It was during the fall, when drinking new wine with slices of onion pie was the tradition. We took them to Kaiserslautern to partake of the custom.

When we returned, we saw that the lace curtains weren't closed as when we left. Something was terribly wrong! We'd had a fire, and the fire department had come to put it out. I went racing to the living room to check on the puppies—they were gone, along with Snoozer, Cinder, and Missy. The neighbor from across the street had noticed smoke coming out one of the windows; his wife had called the fire department while he ran over, lifted our locked garage door, grabbed our fire extinguisher off the wall, and raced upstairs to try to put out the fire.

Everyone in the neighborhood knew we had puppies. They alerted the firemen to get the puppies out; someone called our cleaning lady, who drove over right away. The firemen brought down five little puppies, but our cleaning lady knew one was missing. A fireman raced back upstairs and found the missing puppy, who had stopped breathing. He massaged the puppy's chest and gave him mouth-to-mouth, which started him breathing again. That he managed to breathe life back into the puppy was a miracle.

Having puppies was certainly a learning experience, but we grew tired of all the work. Both females were taken to the Ramstein vet for surgery. They continued to be great friends for almost sixteen years. And they also continued to bring me field mice. The first time or two they would dump them in my lap while I was watching TV or reading. My first inclination was to stand up, knock the mouse to the floor, and scream. They didn't understand what I was upset about; after all, they were very proud of their catch and wanted me to have it. After about two times, they continued bringing me mice but dropped them at my feet. I was happy to praise them for their hunting abilities then.

❦ CHAPTER 21 ❦

Vietnam

LOTS OF RETIRED MILITARY MEN BECOME TEACHERS FOR DoDDS. THEY'RE GREAT role models for the kids, and their discipline is needed these days. One such military man and his wife were regulars for dinner parties at our house. One night eight of us were enjoying a Mexican dinner: chicken and corn soup, enchiladas, guacamole-covered cauliflower, and mousse.

All the men were telling the war stories that never seemed to grow too old to listen to in groups such as ours. Our science teacher and Frank were both telling stories at the same time to different ends of the table. Frank heard part of our friend's and commented that it sounded very similar to his story! As it turned out, they were in the same bar on the same night at the same time the bar was supposed to be blown up.

Don's friends, Vietnamese officers, whispered something, and everybody got up and went out the back exit. A Vietnamese soldier ran into the bar and said something in the local language. Everyone at Frank's table exited the bar by the front door. After both groups had cleared the building and were safely away, the bar blew up!

Our Mexican dinner certainly proved that in the military, it's a very small world. Don has since passed away, but his history remains very unusual. He wanted to be a doctor, but at that time African Americans were not admitted into medical schools unless the family was able to pay the tuition. Don was accepted at a school in England with a full scholarship. All he had to do was pay for the flight over. He had no money so he joined the air force and flew with the Tuscegee Airmen. After retiring as a Lt. Colonel (O5), he became a science teacher for DoDDS. His wife was the head of the English department at the local high school. His five children were all college graduates. The oldest went to medical school and then to law school. His career was Don's dream come true.

❧ CHAPTER 22 ❧
Aunt Vivian

ABOUT THAT TIME, FRANK'S ELDERLY AUNT VIVIAN CAME TO VISIT US. WE'D TRAV-
eled to Frank's home state of Texas to see her before, and we knew she'd love seeing all
the history and sights of Europe. We picked her up at Frankfurt International Airport
in late June; she arrived wearing her infamous three-inch heels and drove Frank crazy
with her several pairs. Aunt Vivian was unbalanced on her heels and unaware of safety
issues with escalators. Frank was always grabbing her elbow to steer her safely away
from obstacles in her path. Because Frank was working and I was going to school to
get certified in gifted education, Aunt Viv selected some countries to visit. Frank put
her on bus trips to Holland, Spain, and Italy. During the weekends at home, we took in
the local sights by car.

Aunt Viv is no longer with us, but she led a very colorful life. She started as the adopted child of another Texas family. She married three times, and all three husbands
were builders. One died after falling off a roof; the second died after a house collapsed
around him, and her last, Uncle Monk, died from smoking.

Aunt Viv was a fun-loving individual, and we gathered lots of stories to tell about
her after she left for Dallas. On her trip through Holland, the bus dropped them off in
downtown Amsterdam to go shopping; they were to meet the bus in two hours at the
front door of the department store where they'd been let out. Apparently Aunt Viv went
out the wrong door and kept walking, looking for the bus or a familiar face. After about
thirty minutes, she had the good sense to realize she was lost and needed some help;
she didn't speak the language, didn't know the name of her hotel because they had not
yet checked into their rooms, and was tired of walking around by herself. The street
was narrow, with lots of store fronts; some would call them window fronts. Scantily
clad, some would say provocative-looking, girls were sitting in the windows for all the
passersby to see. She went into one and said she was lost; the Dutch were certainly
willing to help this white-haired American in her three-inch spikes. The manager called
around to the local hotels usually visited by tourists and, after about four tries, found
her hotel. The manager of the brothel called a taxi and made sure she got in. When she
got to the hotel, she refused to pay the taxi driver. After all, the tour guide had lost her,
so the tour guide was responsible for paying the driver!

Just for your own education: if you are ever on this particular narrow street in

Amsterdam, it's good to know their system. It's similar to the Korean system. If you can see the light, she's free; if there's something in front of the candle, then she's busy!

On another occasion at the same hotel, several of the group were leaving from the entrance at the same time. Outside was a man with a gun, waving it around and pointing it at the passersby. Aunt Viv marched up to the gunman and demanded that he put the gun down and stop making a nuisance of himself. Without her knowledge, the others from her group had formed a *V* behind her; Aunt Viv was at the apex of the *V*!

How do we know so much about Aunt Viv and her tours? That's easy. Do you remember that Frank had to give a lot of information to the military when we decided to get married? His job required security clearance. When Aunt Viv's tour to Holland ended back on Ramstein Air Base, she gave our home phone number to all her newfound friends; she'd also told them his job description was a spy! During the week following the historic bus trip to Amsterdam, some people from the bus called to talk to Aunt Viv. As she was climbing the stairs in her three-inch spikes, the callers would talk to Frank. They thought Frank was so lucky to have Aunt Viv as his adopted aunt; they also related all the escapades she'd gotten into. They loved Aunt Viv, just as we did. Now we love our memories of her and the good stories she gave us to tell our friends.

❧ CHAPTER 23 ❧

Egypt

AFTER AUNT VIVIAN WENT HOME, WE SPENT OUR WEEKENDS TRAVELING AROUND Germany, visiting the museums, the local beer and wine fests, going to military dinners, and so forth for many more years. Then we started visiting Egypt, Israel, Russia, England, Austria, Switzerland, and many others. I had been to all these places, except for Egypt, during my first tour in Grafenwoehr.

Egypt had never been on my list, but it was at the top of Frank's. I'll write about all the strange, funny Egyptian incidents as if they all happened on one trip, but they didn't. We traveled there four or five times, usually during Christmas break, when the temperatures were at their lowest.

Our first trip to Egypt took place about 1985 during Christmas vacation. The weather in Frankfurt was alternating between rain, sleet, and snow, but Cairo was much worse by comparison. Walking outside the airport terminal became the smelliest introduction to any country I'd ever experienced. You got used to the dry, hot Egyptian temperatures, but the smell never went away. When I complained that I wanted to get on a plane and fly back to the much sweeter-smelling Germany, I was rudely reminded that I'd smell bad too if I were more than two thousand years old. After returning to Germany, we finally figured out the cause of the bad smell. For the first couple of days after we'd landed, the clouds had been close to the ground, trapping all the smells close to the ground.

We made several trips to Egypt to explore other pyramids farther south and never experienced the really bad smells again. There was always an odor, just like Korea, but never again were the clouds clinging to the ground! Thank goodness.

We followed in Napoleon's footsteps and climbed to the top of the pyramids. Only one-way traffic was allowed due to the narrow passages. The interiors of the structures were cool, but if you're claustrophobic, admire the pyramids from the outside. Napoleon, like Lord Byron, liked to publicize his historical visits by carving his name somewhere near the top of the pyramid.

Our hotel security service accompanied us to the Sound and Light Show and panicked when they lost us! Frank and I weren't really lost, but the guards lost sight of us. Big smiles broke out when we returned to the spot where they'd parked our security vehicle. We didn't realize they were also heavily armed until we were shopping in the bazaar area. It was warm, but our guard who was built like a football player wore a suit with a long coat. The coat flared open while he was walking, and it was easy to see the Uzi he carried for our protection. We never felt in danger, but a busload of German tourists had been attacked months before. Tourists are a big part of the economy, and the Egyptians were taking the tourist trade seriously.

We left Cairo by plane to fly to a beach resort on the Red Sea. Beach time varies each winter, depending on the local weather. Our intent was to sun for three days and then fly to Luxor and the Valley of the Kings. Our best-laid plans did not see fruition! The cabin we were assigned was not heated, and the temperatures inside rivaled Germany's outside temperature. The wind reminded me of a Florida hurricane or a Pacific typhoon. We left!

We hired a taxi to drive us to Luxor. Our driver drove quickly through the desert, looking in his rearview mirror every few minutes. Frank and I both noticed his strange actions. It didn't take too long for our light bulbs to light up. With all the recent terrorist activities, he was just being a cautious taxi driver. We were very happy to be his passengers; he was concerned about us, although he had no affiliation with our hotel or tour group.

We stayed in the old but quaint Luxor Hotel. The room was just big enough for the bed; if one of us wanted to walk around, the other person had to get out of the way! It wins the award for being the smallest hotel room in my travels around the world!

The room included three meals per day; none were buffet. Dining was a very proper experience. We had a choice of three entrees, which were delivered by waiters in tailor-made white uniforms, complete with jacket and bow tie. The staff must have been trained by the British to work for the aristocracy! It was an experience we enjoyed, and it's never been repeated in any of our many Christmas trips. The Christmas Eve dinner was even more proper and the food even more elaborately garnished. The entrees were what you'd expect for a holiday dinner—fish, turkey, and beef served in generous portions by our extraordinary waiters. We were surprised when it came time for dessert. They had prepared an elaborate array of assorted sweets on a buffet table. We were definitely in heaven that Christmas!

We visited the pool early one morning and watched a worker shinny up a palm tree and cut off the dead fronds. As the fronds fell to the ground, we took mental pictures that we remember every few years. It was a sight we'd never seen before and never have since. We've seen the modern trucks with the basket for the workmen to stand in, but never have we seen a skinny guy shinny up a tree with just a wide rubber band around his hips to hold him safely in place.

Now the Luxor Hotel is gone. Each time we travel there, we look at pictures of hotels, thinking it was maybe sold and renamed, but it's gone. Never again will anyone enjoy the hospitality and beauty of their services.

Riding on a traditional *felucca* (a long and narrow riverboat with sails) is a treat you must try at least once. We once stayed in a hotel on Elephantine Island and had to travel back and forth to the mainland each day. It was the felucca or the ferry. We'd take a bus to the dock, and another bus would pick up us on the other side. It was a fun experience, if you didn't think about the boat overturning or the ferry sinking! Third-world travel does make one think of safety rules and regulations that aren't practiced locally.

Since so much of our travels ended up in the classroom as part of lessons, my history teacher husband had to float down the Nile one December to get to Abu Simbul. As we were leaving Luxor by bus to meet the cruise ship, the bus driver drove us in the wrong direction until he met up with a long line of buses facing the opposite direction. Our bus joined the line, which was led by a military convoy, with more military vehicles interspersed within the line, and the line of buses ended with a military van. We were then escorted to the Nile where the tourist ships were docked.

There are famous temples and pyramids off the Nile River that you can only reach by boat. Our cruise ship was a glorified barge, and all workers were men. Men changed the sheets, served meals, and cleaned the deck. I lost an unopened pair of nylons on that trip. I guess they were destined to be a Christmas present for someone's wife or girlfriend. I wasn't too upset, just surprised, as I'd never been robbed before.

Aswan is easily reached by plane. I don't recommend traveling by land; it would take too long and the ride would be uncomfortable. Below Aswan is a dam built by the Russians. Because of the dam, Abu Simbul and its temples of Ramses II had to be moved from the original site to a higher location. Relocating Abu Simbul was an UNESCO project and it collected coins from children around the world to help fund the project. During my elementary school years I remember collecting dimes for a project, but I'm not sure it was for Abu Simbul. Frank was educated in Chicago, Iowa, and Nebraska, but he collected dimes too. When the dam was flooded, the old site was suddenly underwater. Abu Simbul would have been underwater, too, and not much good as a tourist attraction.

If you love tasting foreign food like I do, eating in Aswan is totally different from Luxor or Cairo. The spices are different, or the measurements for the spices and combinations are different. I never did figure it out, but I'd go back to Aswan anytime just to eat! My husband, who refused to eat eggplant at home, ordered a meal that came with eggplant. He loved his meal, right down to the aubergine; everywhere we've traveled in Europe and Africa eggplant is called aubergine. He insisted that I make the delicious aubergine dish when we got home. No way was I going to spoil his dinner with the truth! When we got home, I bought some aubergine and served it. He figured out what it was right away and reminded me he didn't like eggplant. He didn't intend to eat it! That's when I called his manly bluff. He's eaten aubergine ever since and even grills it during the summer! I have a lot to thank Aswan for.

During the Roman Empire, Alexandria was the second-largest city after Rome. Alexandria had never been on our tours, but they had made some new discoveries in the waters off the port city. We added it to our itinerary, but we had to drive from Cairo. I don't recommend it; the trip is long and bumpy, and there's nothing to see but dust and more dust. Our hotel was nice, and our guide took us to the special restaurants the locals had designated for tourists. Since we don't consider ourselves normal tourists, we went out on our own to sight-see and people-watch.

When we got hungry, we stopped in a large dining area full of restaurants meant for the locals. That was a big mistake for me! I was sick within three hours and for the next three days. The moral of this story was never eat in a local Egyptian restaurant again, no matter how good it looks or how delicious it smells! It was the first and only time I got sick in Egypt. The tourist hotels are safer, and their food is delicious. There are lots of buffets, so you can pick and choose whatever looks or smells good.

Our guide had put together a city tour of Alexandria that was meant to keep us occupied for the full time. We saw the harbor site of Heracleum, the city named after Hercules, but we did so from outside the tent the French had erected around the dig. We did see a wooden sailing ship that had been pulled from the depths of the Mediterranean since the harbor city is now 6.5 kilometers off shore. If you were to travel to Alexandria now, the French have finished this part of their excavation, and the museum has been built around the site.

However, our tour guide didn't plan very well, so he had to come up with something to keep us busy and happy enough to tip him at the end. We were taken to the Jewish temple, which is not open to tourists; it's located inside a very tall wrought-iron fence, the gate guarded by an armed soldier. We were allowed inside to talk with the Jewish woman in charge. She was led outside to meet us by a tall gentleman wearing a suit and tie and carrying an Uzi; she was in her eighties and very frail. It was evident she was revered by the insiders.

She led us into her office and carefully explained to us that only Jews were allowed inside the temple. If we were Jews, then we could visit. We were left with the impression that we could become Jews for a few minutes in return for a contribution. The interior was a sight to behold. She lectured on the history of the church and told us they needed men to fly in from Israel in order to practice the Sabbath. It doesn't happen often, but Israel does send men for important services, like Yom Kippur and Rosh Hashanah.

The Jewish community in Alexandria is almost gone; only a very few older people still live there. When they die, the temple will be closed. Younger people are not immigrating to Egypt these days. Visiting with the old lady was the highlight of our trip to Alexandria; we wonder about her often. I'm sure she's passed by now, but is the temple still open?

Back in Cairo we did the last of our panic buying—that's what you do when you're leaving a country and you think you didn't spend enough money on dust collectors or buy enough clothing, shoes, jewelry, or gold! Frank bought an old perfume bottle etched in gold to share in his classes.

My object of choice caught me by complete surprise. I passed a jewelry store, and something orange caught my eye. I went into the store to question the salesman; he told me it was just a stone found in Egypt. I bought two to make into earrings. A year later, I needed another stone for a matching pendant. A teacher from Mannheim took my order and one earring with her to the same shop. This time my cheap stones were five times as valuable; the guy knew I really wanted it! Now I have earrings and a pendant, made from a stone found only in Egypt, but I still didn't know its true name.

❧ CHAPTER 24 ❧

Turkey

ANOTHER GREAT COUNTRY TO VISIT AND EVEN LIVE IN FOR A COUPLE OF YEARS IS Turkey. A couple of our very good friends often traveled to Turkey; he was there on temporary duty (TDY) quite a bit too. Neither of us had been to Turkey, so we decided to take the leap and try for a military hop. It was our first hop, and everything worked beautifully. We got seats on the flight with no problem, landed in Incirlik on time, and signed up for our return flight a week later.

We took a taxi to a horrible downtown hotel, checked in, and then walked until we found the car rental office. After an hour of haggling with the man, my husband got us a car for the American military price—not the tourist price. We paid about fifty dollars for a week's rental.

That night at the Rose Cafe, which was next door to our horrible hotel, we planned our itinerary. We wanted to see as much as we could in the week we had. We started from Incirlik and drove along the coast toward Antalya. We stopped in Tarsus to see St. Paul's Well. The shopping in Mersin, a port city, is good if you are willing to explore, and the Hilton is a good place to have a meal or to spend the night. We drove through Kizkalesi to Silifke which has a fortress and the Temple of Jupiter. There's also the ferry port to Cyprus. The drive was beautiful. The Mediterranean was turquoise, the sun was shining, the weather was warmer than Germany's April weather, and we were free from kids and Frank's military job for one whole week. The only negative aspect to the drive was the lack of guard rails between the road and the edge of the cliff overlooking the Med. It was a very uncomfortable feeling, not something I'd experienced since Greece and Lord Bryon.

Our first real adventure started when we saw two soldiers walking down the road in front of us. Suddenly they heard our car and indicated they wanted to hitch a ride with us. Their rifles were looking our way but not exactly pointed at us. Frank, being one of our air force's finest, decided to stop. After all, they had the guns!

We knew from our trips to Israel and Egypt that young soldiers in the Middle East keep bullets in their Uzi and are prepared to shoot at the first indication of trouble. We definitely didn't want to start any trouble. I call them young because in our experience only young kids or teenagers are walking around the city streets or in this case country roads with loaded guns. I don't know what the older more mature men were doing as their military jobs.

Frank and the older kid discussed Turkish military life; he owned one hundred acres on each side of the road we were traveling. He asked Frank how much land he owned in his military! When the soldiers reached their destination, they thanked us very nicely for the ride, wished Frank good luck with his military job, and waved good-bye. We returned the wave, gave a big sigh of relief, and continued down the road to Alanya.

After passing Alanya, Frank continued along the Mediterranean until we arrived in Antayla toward evening. We stayed in a brand-new hotel right off the main road. The big hotels and the beach were across the street. We picked the nicest-looking hotel for dinner, but once I noticed the buffet tables, we left to find a fish restaurant. We had a lovely meal and retired for the night. Retiring was easier said than done. The room was freezing and had no heater, the water was cold, and the new furniture was not comfortable.

Needless to say, we were off very early the next morning. After a lunch of pilic (chicken), rice, french fries, shepherd's salad, and beer for the costly sum of $4.00 total, it was my turn to drive. I turned off the main road to find St. Nicholas' birthplace, just as dusk was falling. We started climbing a mountainous trail. As the road without safety rails wound around the mountain, fog began to roll in. What a time for me to be driving! We totally missed St. Nickolas' town. As the fog began to dissipate, the dinky little path through the mountainous area suddenly stopped. In front of us bulldozers were moving dirt, constructing what looked to be the groundwork for a four-lane high-way. We traveled between the trucks and bulldozers for about fifteen miles and came to Kas. There was no way we were going to backtrack the next morning just to find St. Nicholas' birthplace.

We had a great dinner in Kas; a tent area on the beach was filled with little places to sit and eat. The food was displayed around the tables. You could pick your food and have it delivered to your table along with beer or water.

After dinner we decided to hit the road. I was driving. When we saw the road signs for the next town, we decided we didn't want to chance going any farther. The distance was too far for night travel.

We turned around and tried to get a room at a quaint little hotel we'd seen. Evidently, everybody else thought it was quaint too; all five rooms were full. The manager referred us down the street, where we got a room, but we went back to the quaint hotel for drinks. Their bar offered Courvoisier and Drambuie, our favorites!

The next morning we had lots and lots of cold water for our showers and Turkish coffee, hard rolls, tomatoes, and cucumbers for breakfast. We vowed we'd stay in the cute hotel the next time.

We drove inland to Fethiye and saw the pre-Roman Lycian tombs carved into the mountainsides. We stopped to take pictures. When we were ready to leave, our inexpensive rental car couldn't start! The key had broken off in the ignition. We had visions of spending the rest of our vacation waiting for a mechanic. We were wrong—and delighted that we were wrong! A man came within half an hour, removed the broken-off key, and gave us a new key. We were ecstatic. As we drove away, we discovered the tombs were floodlit at night, and the town filled with tourists.

We continued on our way, skipping Marmaris and Bodrum. We didn't need to catch a ferry to Kos, Rhodes, or other Greek islands, so we left them for another trip. We arrived in Kusadasi, which is south of Izmir and Efes, and found a lovely hotel on a cliff above the Mediterranean. We gave it four stars for the room, heater, and hot water, but none for the breakfast. As a matter of fact, we left without eating. The coffee was memorable but not for the right reasons.

We wanted to tour Efes, or Ephesus, built by the Greeks, one of the seven churches cited in the Book of Revelation, which flourished when conquered by the Roman Empire. The Gospel of John is thought to have been written there. Paul lived in Ephesus, teaching and providing missionary services to inner Turkey. Today only 15 percent of the city has been excavated.

We've been back to Ephesus many times, and each time more and more of the old city has been brought back to life. The marble streets are a sight to see, along with the famous library and amphitheater. Seniors from Izmir High School were lucky—graduation was held at Efes. Imagine having your graduation pictures taken in front of the library.

Mary's house was also on our list of places to stop. When we parked at Mary's, there were soldiers everywhere. They didn't try to hinder us in any way, so we kept walking. As we were leaving the area, we walked close to a group of bodyguards surrounding a Turkish general. The general spoke to us, so we stopped. He and Frank had a great conversation about our army and his army, and then we said good-bye.

Our next stop was Izmir, which has become my favorite Turkish city. We did a little sightseeing; just enough to make it clear we needed to come back another time.

In Pamukkale, north of Denizli, we encountered the therapeutic Travertine hot springs, with rock formations from deposits in the water. People have used the pools for thousands of years. The old Roman baths in the museum are visited by tourists from all over the world. Nowadays there are hotels near the site.

In Cappadocia, we visited Goreme, which is famous for the fairy chimneys in the Goreme Open-Air Museum. People lived in the rock houses, hiding from Romans soldiers and other conquerors. You can rent a cave as your hotel if you so desire.

Konya is the home of the whirling dervishes. As we drove toward Konya, we passed the Turkish version of the Grand Canyon. What a beautiful sight! We spent the night in a hotel just one level nicer than the horrible one in Adana; this one had no stars either. As a matter of fact, at that time, none of the hotels in the little cities had stars, just the big cities—Izmir, Istanbul, and Ankara.

The night before our morning military hop, we arrived late back in Adana. We stayed in the same hotel and went next-door for dinner. We turned in our rental with twelve hundred additional miles on its odometer. We were sore, tired, and dirty but happy with our seven-day trip.

The Rose Cafe was memorable; not only did it share my name, but I was the only female in the place both times. The men stared at us, of course. They drank their *raki*, the national liqueur, and drank their national beer, Efes. We had another wonderful chicken shish kebab with one scoop of sticky rice, one pile of french fries, and the best salad ever. Our meals in Turkey were always the same; chicken (pilic) was the only word we recognized!

On our travels through the country, we'd always stopped for lunch at truck stops. Not only was their food the best, it was the only place we dared to stop; there were always lots of trucks there. Meals for two with an Efes beer cost us somewhere between four and five dollars. If you love salad, go to a Turkish restaurant and ask for a shepherd's salad. The pilic shish kebab was always fresh; not only could you taste the freshness, but sometimes you found chicken feathers! They were probably being raised right out back.

If you've never traveled to a third-world country like Korea or Turkey, a word of warning to the ladies. Don't go into a bathroom unless it's in your hotel. You won't enjoy the experience.

The roads in Turkey were atrocious. It took us awhile to understand the significance of the piles of rocks we'd see on the highways. They were stacked on top of each other and were tall enough for drivers to notice from a distance. It was a warning that potholes were ahead so drivers could reduce speed. Some roads looked recently paved, but due to the rain and the poor quality of the paving materials, big holes would appear.

We loved meeting the Turkish people; everyone was friendly and wanted to talk about America. If we needed help, we tried using our German, and that seemed to work. With our leather jackets we looked German anyway. Using German to communicate was helpful, but we were careful to let them know that we were *not* German. They hate the Germans. If you're German, the price goes up for items you might be trying to buy. Schliemann stole artifacts and entire temples from Turkey during the WWI and shipped them to Germany. If you've been in the Pergamon Museum in Berlin, you can see the entire temple of Pergamon, which was taken down piece by piece, transported to Berlin, and rebuilt. The museum walls were constructed around the temple. It's a great museum to visit and is always first on our list when we go to Berlin.

We flew back to Ramstein Air Base right on time, returned to work on Monday, and regaled our friends who'd recommended Turkey with our stories. When they asked what we'd bought, Frank and I just looked at each other. We hadn't bought anything! No leather, no carpets, no gold, no spices, no copper or brass—not anything!! We had spent a total of $1,000 for our week's adventure, exactly what we'd planned. We'd driven our American-priced rental two thousand kilometers, about twelve hundred miles. It remains one of our most favorite trips. We reminisce frequently about the people, especially the soldiers and their land.

We've been back to Turkey many times since. And, yes, we did buy, buy, buy. We own carpets, gold jewelry, leather, and copper, and lots of spices litter my kitchen cabinets. Saffron and cumin were my favorites to buy, along with bars of olive-oil soap. You can tell the soap is genuine because of the flecks of black olives in the soap.

We now understand why they plant orange trees on the sides of their four-lane boulevards. I could never understand why people left the oranges on the trees. They looked free for the taking … well, they're sour oranges! They're grown to sell to England for making orange marmalade.

❧ C H A P T E R 2 5 ❧
More Travels in Turkey

ON ONE OF OUR VISITS, WE PLANNED TO STAY IN OUR FRIENDS' APARTMENT WHILE they were on leave in the States. We landed at Incirlik Air Force Base, rented a car, and headed to Ankara to visit the archeological museum we'd missed on our first trip. We spent the night in the Etap Hotel but ate breakfast the next morning in a little restaurant next door. The tomatoes must have been past their prime. We both got sick, Frank more so than I. We barely made it to the outskirts of Izmir before the chills and fever hit us. We didn't know where the apartment was, but we took the turn for the harbor. We ended up driving right through their bazaar; once you turned into it, there was nowhere to turn around nor any left or right turns that would lead you out again! We received lots of angry looks, and who could blame them?

Finally, our nightmare ended. We came to a four-lane avenue and followed it to the nearest hotel. We checked into the Efes Hotel and collapsed. The next morning we found our friends' apartment, which was right across the street from the Efes Hotel! The houseboy was working when we made it to the fifth floor; we found the bedroom and collapsed again. Sometime later that afternoon, we managed to drag ourselves out of bed; our goal was to find the American hospital and see an American doctor. The houseboy took us to the kitchen balcony and pointed to the hospital. It was right next door, but the entrance was on the street parallel to the apartment's entrance. What a miracle! We were pronounced sick, with a chance of recovering in about two or three weeks. The physician recommended his favorite medicine for newcomers; we took the medicine religiously, slept most of the day, and got up just to eat. Then it was back to sleeping again.

After about a week, Ramadan began, so that added to our predicament. Some restaurants close by wouldn't open until sundown; we found an Italian restaurant that served lots of different choices and was open earlier. We started feeling almost normal, so we decided to go to Rhodes to escape Ramadan. We had ridden the Turkish buses before, so we knew we needed to buy our tickets in advance so that we could get the two seats right inside the door. Turkish buses in those days weren't air-conditioned, and the drivers drove with the doors open. We traveled in style, cool as cucumbers, but those behind us didn't fare as well. We made it to Bodrum and took the ferry across to

Rhodes. The ferry ride was cool from the sea breezes, but it did not prepare us for the heat on Rhodes.

We loved the Greek food; it was a welcome change from Turkish Italian spaghetti or lasagna! But it was summer, which meant the temperature hovered around 100 F. It was too hot to think, much less enjoy the sights. We drank lots of water and beer, ate cold salads with feta cheese chased by lusciously sweet watermelon, and vegetated. After about three days, we'd had enough of Greece and went back to our air-conditioned apartment in Izmir.

While staying in Izmir, we spent money on souvenirs. We bought some carpets that the shopkeeper packaged up for mailing. We used the army post office (APO) address and insured them. After spending about six weeks in Turkey, we went home to wait for our treasures to arrive.

Several days later, we unpacked our carpets and just stared at them. Did we really buy these ugly wool throw rugs? They weren't the same as we remembered. Had our sickness caused us to buy such awful examples of Hereke and Anatolian tribal rugs? After we got over the shock, we decided the merchant had substituted our rugs for some cheaper models.

Thanksgiving break arrived, and we flew to Izmir to visit our friends. Their son was a kindergarten student, and we became his Show and Tell item for the week. That was a new experience for me; I had started my teaching career as a kindergarten teacher. Show and Tell is a very big deal for five-year-olds!

We had mailed our rugs back to our friends, so we were ready to return to the carpet dealer. We took our base commander friend with us. We got our refund and went to a more reputable carpet dealer, Roza's Carpets. We were the talk of the market for weeks. Lots of Americans buy carpets but no one returns them like we did. Most buyers are back in the States when they realize something is wrong.

The Heiecks, who owned our favorite restaurant in Weilerbach, called the Dorfschenke, saw our carpets from Roza and asked us to buy them one on our next trip to Turkey. They told us their price range and the color. We picked out the carpet for them and brought it home on the plane with us. They loved it.

We spent every Friday night at the Heiecks's German restaurant for years. They had a salad bar long before the other restaurants knew what one was. My favorite meal was the Holzfaller steak, a bone-in pork steak with a spicy marinade, with potatoes fried in bacon grease. It's hard to find it in a restaurant these days. You have to buy them and grill them yourself.

We recommend Roza to all our friends. When she opened a store in the Ramstein area, she and her husband started receiving invitations to our parties. It's nice when Turkish merchants move into your geographic area. Shopping is so much more fun, with no mailing to do, no problems getting cash from the local Turkish bank, and no insurance problems. Roza will even let you take a carpet home to try out for a while. If you don't like it after you see it with your furniture, you can return it and try something else. Dealing with Roza and her husband, Adnon, is a pleasurable experience. Now she's branched out into Pashmina scarves. She gets them from India, China, and Turkey. They're a great buy and excellent gifts for Christmas or birthdays.

If you're like me, you prepare a recipe the way it's written the first time; then you start changing it by adding ingredients, spices, or amounts. Here are just a few of our favorite dishes from our time in the Ramstein area.

Beer Chicken

Ingredients
    1 medium onion, chopped
    2 tablespoons butter
    1 can tomato soup
    2/3 cup beer
    1 teaspoon curry powder
    ½ teaspoon oregano
    Dash pepper
    3 skinless, boneless chicken breasts
    ¼ cup Parmesan cheese

Directions
Using a medium saucepan, sauté onion in butter until tender.

Add tomato soup, beer, curry, oregano, and pepper. Stir, bring to a boil, and then let simmer, uncovered, 10 minutes. The smell will drive you crazy!

Arrange chicken in large rectangular pan. Pour tomato mixture over chicken. The soup mixture makes a great gravy for rice or mashed potatoes.

Bake beer chicken, uncovered, @ 350 F for 50 minutes. Sprinkle with cheese.

Barbecued Brisket

(An old recipe from Frank's family)

Ingredients
  7 pounds beef brisket for grilling

Sauce
  2 cups catsup
  3 tablespoons whole mustard seeds
  1 cup water
  1 tablespoon paprika
  2 onions, chopped
  2 teaspoons oregano
  ½ cup red wine vinegar
  2 teaspoons chili powder
  ½ cup oil
  ½ teaspoon salt
  3 tablespoons brown sugar
  ½ teaspoon ground cloves
  3 tablespoons Worcestershire sauce
  ½ teaspoons garlic powder

Directions
Wrap 7 pounds beef brisket in heavy-duty aluminum foil and grill on low heat for one hour.

Sauce
Add all ingredients to a 2-quart saucepan and simmer for 30 minutes, uncovered.

Using an electric slicer, cut meat into slices and place in large rectangular pan (lasagna size). Pour sauce over meat, cover pan with foil, and bake in 300 F-oven for one hour. The meat will finish cooking in the oven. The longer it stays in the oven, the more tender it is. Leftovers can be frozen.

Beer Marinade for Flank or Skirt Steak

Ingredients
¼ cup olive oil
¼ cup fresh lemon juice
1 cup beer
2 cloves garlic, crushed
1 teaspoon salt
1 bay leaf
¼ teaspoon pepper
½ teaspoon dry mustard
½ teaspoon basil
½ teaspoon oregano

1-1/2 pound flank or skirt steak

Directions
Blend all marinade ingredients.

Add beef to a large rectangular pan; pour marinade over steak. Pierce steak with fork. Turn steak over in marinade. Pierce second side and turn over again.

Cover with plastic wrap and put in refrigerator for 3–4 hours. Turn meat over about every hour to make sure both sides are soaking equally.

Grill to taste. Use electric knife and slice into thin strips. Reheat leftover sauce and pour over meat. Serve immediately; meat cools quickly.

Black Russian Cake

Ingredients
    1 package yellow cake mix
    ½ cup sugar
    1 (6-ounce) chocolate instant pudding
    1 cup oil
    4 eggs
    ¼ cup vodka
    ¼ cup Kahlua
    ¾ cup water

Topping
    ½ cup powdered sugar
    ¼ cup Kahlua

Directions
Combine all ingredients in a large bowl.

Mix on low speed for 1 minute; then beat at medium speed for 4 minutes.

Spoon into greased and floured 10-inch Bundt pan.

Bake 350 F for 1 hour; use toothpick to test if done. Cool 10 minutes.

Invert on a cake plate. Pierce with fork.

Combine powdered sugar and Kahlua in bowl; mix well with fork.

Drizzle over cake.

We planted several different berries in our backyard in Germany. The blackberries were always very prolific, and we used this recipe a lot. We like it best warm from the oven, served with ice cream or whipped cream.

Blackberry Cobbler

Ingredients
   ¾ cup sugar
   1/3 cup flour
   ½ teaspoon cinnamon
   4 cups blackberries
   1 cup oatmeal
   1 stick butter, melted and cooled

Directions
Preheat oven to 350 F.

Mix sugar, flour, and cinnamon in a 3 quart mixing bowl.

Gently stir in blackberries.

Lightly spray loaf pan (9 ¼ x 5 ¼ x 2 ¾) with oil. Pour batter into a loaf pan.

Mix oatmeal and butter. Spread on top of blackberries.

Bake 30 minutes at 350 F. Serves 6–8.

Serve warm with whipped cream or vanilla ice cream.

Calico Salad

Ingredients

    20 ounces frozen mixed vegetables, defrosted and drained
    10 ounces frozen baby lima beans, defrosted and drained
    ¼ cup onion, chopped
    ½ cup celery, chopped
    ½ cup green bell pepper, chopped
    1 small can black olives, chopped
    1/3 small head of cauliflower, cut into flowerettes

Marinade

    1 package ranch dressing, dry
    1 cup mayonnaise

Directions

Note: There's no need to cook the frozen vegetables since they have already been cooked at the factory.

Mix all ingredients together in a large bowl, cover with plastic wrap, and let the ranch dressing work its magic overnight in refrigerator.

Stir to refresh its appearance before serving. Great for cookouts!

Chicken Diablo

Ingredients

    6 boneless, skinless chicken breasts
    1 can mushroom soup
    ¾ cup mild salsa
    1 tablespoon peppercorns
    1 teaspoon garlic powder
    ¼ teaspoon cumin
    1 stalk celery, chopped
    1 can artichoke hearts, drained, quartered
    1 carrot, chopped
    1 small onion, chopped
    1 small can sliced black olives, drained and sliced
    chopped cilantro for garnishing

Directions

Arrange chicken in 9-x-13-inch baking dish. Bake at 350 F for 20 minutes.

While chicken is baking, mix soup, salsa, peppercorns, garlic, and cumin. Add chopped celery, carrot, and onion.

Arrange artichokes around chicken in the baking dish, pour soup mixture over chicken and artichokes. Sprinkle top with sliced olives. Bake for another 25–30 minutes, until chicken is no longer pink.

Garnish with chopped cilantro. Serve with sticky rice.

Rose Porter

This easy recipe was of the first desserts I made after getting married.

Chocolate Mousse

Serves 4

Ingredients
> 1 teaspoon unflavored gelatin
> 1 tablespoon cold water
> 2 tablespoons boiling water
> ½ cup sugar
> ¼ cup cocoa
> 1 teaspoon vanilla
> 1 cup heavy cream, very cold

Directions
Sprinkle gelatin over cold water in small bowl. Stir and let stand 1 minute to soften.

Add boiling water. Stir until gelatin is completely dissolved.

Stir together sugar and cocoa in small cold mixer bowl. Add heavy cream and vanilla.

Beat at a medium speed until stiff peaks form. Pour in gelatin mixture and beat until well blended.

Spoon into serving dishes. Chill for 30 minutes.

Note: To double recipe, use 1 envelope gelatin and double remaining ingredients.

If you're looking for a party or housewarming present, here's an easy one; just write down the recipe and add the basic ingredients to a baggie and put in a basket or decorative jar. I used to give this to the office staff and fellow teachers at Christmas time. It sure beats baking dozens and dozens of Christmas cookies!

Confetti Bean Soup

Ingredients
>   8 cups water
>   2 cups mixed beans
>   2 carrots, chopped
>   2 stalks celery, chopped
>   1 medium onion, chopped
>   2 teaspoons chicken bouillon
>   ¼ teaspoon cumin
>   ¼ teaspoon garlic powder
>   2 pounds ham hocks

Directions
Heat water and beans to boiling and cook for 2 minutes. Remove from heat, cover, and let stand one hour. Drain water from beans and add 8 fresh cups water.

Stir in carrots, celery, and onion. Add bouillon, cumin, garlic, and ham hocks. Heat to boiling; simmer for two hours, covered.

Remove hocks and cut meat into chunks. Stir ham into soup.
Serve hot with crackers or chunks of fresh French bread. Leftovers are even better; make it the day before, store in the fridge, and skim off the fat the next day.

Rose Porter

Cucumber Salad

Ingredients
    2 tablespoons sugar
    ½ cup vinegar
    ½ cup water
    ¼ teaspoon salt
    2 medium cucumbers, peeled and sliced
    1 small onion, thinly sliced

Directions
Mix sugar and vinegar, add water and salt.

Add cucumbers and onion slices.

Refrigerate at least 2 hours before serving.

Drain and serve.

I grew up eating this meatloaf. I have no idea where my mother got the recipe. I've substituted barbecue sauce for the steak sauce which also works well.

Delicious Meat Loaf

Ingredients
    1-1/2 pounds ground sirloin
    1 egg, beaten
    1 cup fresh bread crumbs
    3 tablespoons steak sauce
    ¼ teaspoon salt
    dash pepper

Directions
Preheat oven to 350 F.

Mix all ingredients with hands.

Lightly grease loaf pan. Put mixture in pan, add more steak sauce on top, and bake for one hour.

Pour off fat.

Allow to rest for 10 minutes before slicing.

Serves 6–8. Leftovers make great sandwiches!

Easy Chili

Ingredients
   1 pound ground sirloin
   1 small onion, chopped
   1 can (15 ounces) red kidney beans
   1 can (15 ounces) chopped tomatoes
   1 taco seasoning mix (1 ounce)

Directions
Fry sirloin and onion until meat is no longer pink.

Add beans, tomatoes, and taco mix.

Bring to a boil. Simmer for 30 minutes.

Best made a day ahead of serving. Add another can kidney beans to leftovers to extend the amount.

Emerald Punch

Makes 5-1/2 quarts

Ingredients

    46 ounces unsweetened pineapple juice, chilled

    24 ounces limeade concentrate, thawed

    ¼ cup honey

    1 quart gin

    84 ounces 7-Up, chilled

Directions

Combine pineapple juice and limeade in punch bowl.

Add honey and stir. If a tart punch is desired, omit honey.

Add gin, then 7-Up. Add few drops green food coloring if desired.

Add ice to taste.

Italian Veggie Salad

Ingredients
    4 ounces fresh mushrooms, sliced, or a small can
    1 can yellow beans, drained
    1 can green beans, drained
    1 can red kidney beans, drained, rinsed
    1 onion, sliced into rings
    1 green bell pepper, sliced into rings
    1 head iceberg lettuce, torn into pieces
    2 ounces Italian dressing

Directions
Mix all ingredients. Toss with Italian dressing right before serving.

A bag of mixed salad greens works well in place of the iceberg lettuce.

My husband loves this!

Mandarin Orange Salad

Ingredients
    8 ounces Cool Whip, thawed
    Small box orange Jello (0.3 ounce)
    1 can mandarin oranges, drained
    1 large can crushed pineapple, drained (20 ounces)

Directions
Mix Jello with oranges until lightly blended. Add pineapple. Fold Cool Whip into mixture. Refrigerate for 4 hours.

Recipe can be doubled for a larger crowd. Sour cream can be substituted for the Cool Whip.

Rose Porter

Mexican Lasagna

Ingredients
- 1-1/2 cups ricotta cheese
- 1 tablespoon Italian seasoning
- 1-1/2 teaspoons dried parsley flakes
- 4 ounces fresh mushrooms, sliced
- 1 cup fresh Parmesan, grated
- Your favorite chili recipe, already prepared, about 5 cups
- 8 ounces thin, no-precooking lasagna noodles
- 2-1/2 cups mozzarella cheese, shredded

Lasagna directions

Preheat oven to 350 F. In a large bowl, mix ricotta, Italian seasoning, parsley, mushrooms, and Parmesan cheese.

Lightly spray a rectangular baking pan with oil. Spread a cup of chili on the bottom. Layer noodles, lasagna mixture, chili mixture, and mozzarella cheese.

Bake 40 minutes or until thoroughly heated. Cheese should be nicely browned.

Serves 6–8. Serve with garlic bread and a green salad.

New York–Style Cherry Cheesecake (my favorite!)

Ingredients

Crust

    1-1/2 cups graham cracker crumbs

    ½ cup white sugar

    ¼ cup butter, melted

Filling

    5 (8-ounce) package cream cheese, softened

    5 eggs

    2 egg yolks

    1-3/4 cups white sugar

    1/8 cup flour

    ¼ cup heavy cream

Topping

    2 cans cherry pie filling

Directions

Preheat oven to 400 F. Mix the graham cracker crumbs, ½ cup sugar, and butter together. Press mixture into bottom of a 9- or 10-inch Springform pan.

In a large bowl, combine cream cheese, eggs, and egg yolks. Mix until smooth. Add the remaining 1 ¾ cup white sugar, flour, and heavy cream. Blend until smooth. Pour batter into pan over crust.

Bake at 400 F for 10 minutes. Then turn temperature down to 200 F and continue baking for 1 hour, or until filling is set. Let cheesecake cool completely. Spread two cans of cherry pie filling on top. Cover with plastic wrap and refrigerate.

Cherry Pie Salad/Dessert

Ingredients
    1 large tub Cool Whip, thawed
    1 can sweetened condensed milk
    1 large can crushed pineapple, drained
    1 can mandarin oranges, drained
    4 ounces coconut
    1 can cherry pie filling
    ½ to 1 cup walnuts, chopped

Directions
Mix all ingredients together in large bowl. Cover with plastic wrap and put in refrigerator overnight. Good for cookouts or potlucks.

Rum and Chocolate Cake

Ingredients

Cake

   1 chocolate cake mix
   1 instant chocolate pudding mix, small
   4 eggs
   ½ cup rum
   ½ cup water
   ½ cup oil
   ½ cup slivered almonds

Filling

   2 cups heavy cream
   1/3 cup unsweetened cocoa
   ½ cup powdered sugar
   1 teaspoon vanilla
   ½ cup rum

Directions

Preheat oven to 350 F. Grease and flour two 9-inch layer cake pans. Combine all cake ingredients together in large bowl. Blend well. Then beat at medium mixer speed for 2 minutes. Pour into prepared pans. Cool in pans 10 minutes. Remove and finish cooling on wire racks. Split layers in half.

Filling

Combine all ingredients, except rum, in large mixer bowl. Beat until stiff. Fold in rum. Spread 1 cup filling between each layer and over top.
Store in refrigerator. Serve cold.

This cake is probably the favorite of Frank's poker buddies!

Rum and Walnut Cake

Ingredients
    1 cup walnuts, chopped
    1 package yellow cake mix
    1 instant vanilla pudding mix, small
    4 eggs
    ½ cup cold water
    ½ cup oil
    ½ cup rum

Topping
    ¼ pound butter
    ¼ cup water
    1 cup sugar
    ½ cup rum

Directions
Preheat oven to 325 F. Grease and flour tube or Bundt pan.
Sprinkle nuts over bottom of pan. Mix all cake ingredients together. Pour batter over nuts.

Bake 1 hour. Cool completely before inverting cake onto plate.
Prick top and sides with toothpick.

Topping
Melt butter in saucepan. Stir in water and sugar. Boil 5 minutes, stirring constantly. Remove from heat. Stir in rum.

Spoon and brush topping over top and sides. Allow cake to absorb topping. Repeat until mix is gone.

Spaghetti Salad

Ingredients

    1 pound thin or angel-hair spaghetti, broken into thirds, cooked

    8 ounces Italian dressing

    1 can (14 ounces) artichokes, drained and quartered

    1 large can pitted ripe olives, halved

    ¾ cup green pepper, chopped

    8 ounces cherry tomatoes, halved

    ½ cup Parmesan cheese

    ¼ cup Salad Supreme seasoning

    1 teaspoon basil

    1 teaspoon garlic powder

    ½ teaspoon salt

Directions

Mix everything together and refrigerate 2 days prior to serving. Chilling is mandatory; it enables all the seasonings to mingle with the pasta and veggies.

Stir everything right before serving. Great for cookouts or potlucks.

Rose Porter

Taco Pie

Ingredients
    Frozen pie crust shell, deep-dish style, or make your own
    1 pound ground sirloin
    1 onion, chopped
    1 package taco mix
    1 can refried beans
    1/3 cup taco sauce; I use mild, but hotter might match your family's taste buds.
    2 cups cheddar cheese, shredded

Toppings
    Nacho chips (½ bag), crushed
    Chopped tomatoes (3 large)
    Shredded lettuce (½ head)
    Taco sauce—mild, medium, or hot

Directions
Preheat oven to 400 F. Thaw pie crust for 10 minutes. Then prick bottom and sides with fork. Bake pie shell for 10 minutes.
Remove from oven, and reduce heat to 350 F.

In frying pan, cook ground sirloin and onion until beef is browned. Add taco mix to sirloin and stir. In a bowl mix refried beans and 1/3 cup taco sauce.

Layer half the bean mixture on bottom of pie crust. Top with meat and 1 cup cheddar cheese. Repeat layer. Bake 20–25 minutes, or until cheese is melted and bubbly.

Slice pie. Add toppings to each slice. Serves four generously.

Texas Beans

Ingredients
   2 slices bacon
   1 medium onion, chopped
   1 teaspoon chili powder
   1 can (16-ounces) pork and beans
   1 can (4-ounces) diced green chili peppers
   1 tablespoon catsup
   1 tablespoon molasses
   1 tablespoon hot sauce
   1 tablespoon prepared mustard

Directions
Fry bacon until crisp. Save bacon grease. Drain bacon on paper towels; crumble and set aside.

Cook chopped onion in one tablespoon bacon grease until brown. Add chili powder and cook for one minute.

Stir in the other ingredients, add crumbled bacon, and bring to a boil. Reduce heat and simmer for one hour. Stir occasionally.

These can be served cold or warm. I usually serve warm and add more hot sauce! Great for a cookout!

Rose Porter

My aunt had four kids, and she made this anytime she needed something to fill them up.

Tuna Slaw

Ingredients
> 16-ounce can tuna, packed in water, drained
> 2 cups cabbage, shredded
> 1 carrot, shredded
> 1-1/2 cups cooked macaroni
> 1 small onion, chopped
> ½ cup mayonnaise
> 3 tablespoons prepared mustard
> ½ teaspoon salt
> 1 teaspoon vinegar

Directions
In a large bowl, flake tuna with a fork. Add cabbage, carrot, macaroni, and onion. Stir together.

Mix mayonnaise, mustard, salt, and vinegar in a small bowl.
Pour mixture over macaroni mixture. Stir together. If salad is drier than you like, add more mayonnaise or mustard.

Another great recipe for a cookout or potluck.

My mother used to bake the Tunnel of Fudge. I haven't made it in years because her recipe called for a dry fudge frosting mix which was too hard to find. The last time I made it, I used a readymade frosting. It was just as delicious made with the readymade mix.

Tunnel of Fudge Cake

Ingredients
    1 ½ C butter, softened
    1 ½ C sugar
    6 eggs
    2 C all-purpose flour
    1 container readymade chocolate frosting
    2 C walnuts, chopped

Directions
Preheat oven to 350 F. Grease and flour a Bundt pan.

In a large bowl, cream butter. Add eggs one at a time, beating well after each.

Gradually add sugar, creaming until light and fluffy.

Stir in flour first, and then the frosting, until well blended.

The nuts should be added last.

Pour into pan. Bake for 60-65 minutes.

The center will be gooey, like fudge.
Cool 1 hour on wire rack.

Invert and let cake slide out onto cake plate when it's ready.

If desired, serve warm with vanilla ice cream or whipped cream. I prefer it cold; it's chewier and more like a gooey brownie!

✦ CHAPTER 26 ✦

June 1993
Moving To Turkey

THE WEATHER IN GERMANY IS AN ACQUIRED TASTE. AFTER ELEVEN YEARS, THE NAtive Floridian genes in me required a warmer, sunnier climate. We took the leap and asked for a transfer to Turkey. I received the orders in early June. Frank had retired from the Air Force by then. He was certified to teach K through 12, had a counseling degree, and had completed his internship at my school. He went to Turkey as my dependent and sought a job at the high school.

The stories about health care were atrocious. According to our sources, the vet clinics in America were cleaner than the Turkish hospitals. Turkey didn't have vet clinics for your pets. There were no kennels for boarding them if you wanted to travel and see the sights. You either lived on base and begged your neighbors to look after your pets or hired a maid to take care of them. That was not good news for us.

I believed the health-care horror stories. I made Frank promise me that if I were in an accident or really sick, he would medivac me to Switzerland, Austria, or Germany. I'd even go so far as to accept a hospital in Italy or Spain—anything but a Turkish one! Luckily for me, he never had to fulfill that promise. The worst health issue either of us had was eating the wrong food. Minor stomach problems remained minor.

We had two miniature salt-and-pepper schnauzers and two cats: one perfect male German farm cat and one obnoxious city-cat female. Panic set in. We couldn't just fly to Adana with four animals, without a place to live and no maid for animal-sitting.

We decided to scout the area out in June. As soon as school was out, we flew on a military hop down to Adana, stayed in the same no-star hotel, which reeked of cigarette smoke, and started looking for a place to live. I wanted to live downtown in the middle of all the action; Frank wanted to live out by the lake. Unfortunately for me, there were no empty apartments downtown, and the Turks were building like crazy by the lake. We found an apartment in a new high-rise building, complete with an elevator. It sounds great, doesn't it? Never, never move into a brand-new Turkish apartment building! Nothing works as it should. But I'm getting ahead of myself.

The landlord was very nice. We paid our deposit, gave him our August arrival date, made arrangements for a wrought-iron security door to be installed on our front door, ordered screens to be installed during the summer on our eight balconies, arranged for lace curtains with solid white privacy drapes to be made by the local curtain maker he'd recommended, and so forth. It was so hot in June we had to visit food stores about every two hours to buy more cold water or diet drinks to keep ourselves hydrated. But we were determined to be ready for life in Turkey when we arrived with the four animals.

While we were on the base to catch our military flight back to Ramstein, we went by the school. I requested that a gate pass be waiting for us when we arrived in August. We learned in August *that* turned out to be a joke. Without the gate pass, you'll never get on a military base to obtain a permanent pass or to go shopping or to work.

❧ CHAPTER 27 ❧

August 1993
Moving Day

WE PACKED OUT, SHIPPED FRANK'S NEW TOYOTA CAMRY, AND FLEW ON A NONSTOP flight from Frankfurt to Istanbul. We arrived with the four animals in good health and waited for our luggage so that we could transfer to the local flight to Ankara and then Adana. Because we were going straight to the apartment, we had packed a litter box with a small bag of litter and food for all four animals, plus sheets, towels, and a bar of soap. We shipped our Korean *yo* so that we'd have a bed until our furniture could be delivered. The suitcases contained the rest of our items. The suitcases arrived on the trolley. We kept waiting for the other items ... They never arrived. They'd been lost on a nonstop flight! We demanded and got a hotel room for the night from the airlines, thinking the missing items would arrive the next day.

We found a taxi to take us to the hotel. Taxis are small in Turkey, not the large Mercedes we had in Europe. I wanted to hire two taxis, but Frank wanted to give the driver a chance to figure it out. The large suitcases wouldn't fit into the trunk. They used bungee cords to hold the trunk lid almost closed. Then our driver and another driver looked at the four animal cages and tried to fit them into the small taxi. Two fit in the front seat; Frank and I could squeeze into the back seat with our little bags, but where were the cats going to travel? That was the $64,000 question.

When it sounded like the drivers wanted to hang the cats in their cages off the back of the car, attached to the luggage somehow, I lost control. That was the end of my patience. So we hired two taxis to take us to the hotel. Even with both taxis, it was crowded. We arrived at a very nice four-star hotel located on the beach and checked in. We had no litter box for the cats, so the bellboy found us a box. Frank proceeded to tear up toilet paper into tiny pieces until we thought the cats would be satisfied.

Then we went to the dining room for our meal which was included with our hotel room. We'd already eaten a delicious salmon meal in our upgraded seats in business class and didn't need more food. So we ordered chicken dinners and a bottle of wine. We drank the wine and cut the chicken dinners into bite-size pieces. Later we fed the chicken to the animals. The waiters were appalled, but we had to feed our pets.

The next morning we arrived at the airport for our continuing flight, fully expecting to see our missing items. We were optimistic—but our luggage remained in Frankfurt. There went our best-laid plans for an easy transition to life in Turkey!

We flew on to Ankara and caught our last flight of the day with time to spare. We boarded the Adana plane, and airport workers loaded all four animals inside the cabin with us. We could see them, and they knew we were close by; that helped ease the animals' nervousness, especially the cats.

When we landed, we went straight to our familiar smelly hotel next to the Rose Cafe. We'd enjoyed our first chicken shish meal in Adana there, all the men sipping their raki and drinking their beer, all the while watching the two crazy Americans who liked the Rose Cafe so much they kept coming back again and again.

The extra plus you get flying back and forth to the States or to Turkey from Europe is the miles you accumulate. We earned so many miles we were able to upgrade to business class many times. That certainly made the expense of living so far from home easier to bear. Teaching for the military schools is still an expensive venture, especially if you're traveling with children or a handicapped parent, as some teachers do.

❖ CHAPTER 28 ❖

August 1991–June 1993
Our New Home

THE NEXT MORNING WE WENT TO THE BASE TO BUY SOME ESSENTIALS FOR THE apartment. However, our requested gate pass was not waiting for us. I called the school; my new assistant principal came down to the shopping street to find us. We weren't too hard to locate; he just asked the merchants if they'd seen two new-looking Americans. He brought us dog and cat food and an American bar of soap which we needed. We were ready to head to our new apartment.

We left the four animals and luggage at the smelly hotel and went to pick up our keys. We discovered that all the items we'd requested for our apartment had been installed in the wrong apartment, one located on the ground floor. We wanted to be higher for security reasons. The lucky renters would end up with our screens and security door for free! By this time, we were ready to run away to the Hilton Hotel in Mersin, but instead we started moving into the new apartment, without screens to keep the mosquitoes and bugs out, no curtains to allow us privacy, and no security door.

In Turkey the first person to move into a new apartment buys and installs the tracks for curtains. The first tenant has the marble floors cleaned and polished. The first residents pay to have dirt hauled upstairs for the eight planters, which are at least two feet deep. The poor men who hauled the heavy dirt were not allowed by the on-site building manager to use the elevator; they had to climb the stairs.

We had ceiling fans with lights installed in all the rooms. We found a maid who would help keep the fur from the cats and dogs under control. Our furniture was delivered, and the base delivered the kitchen appliances. We had to buy a washer and dryer. It was 110 degrees in the shade, but the local military store was out of air conditioners! The next delivery date was far into the future. We opted to buy from the Turkish store; we ordered two *White* reversible cold- and hot-air units. Those came from Istanbul in about five days. We were in the apartment, along with workmen, finishing screens, hanging curtains, and installing air conditioners. We were still not cooking at home; it was cheaper and easier to just eat out, so we did. Between the extreme heat and the stress of getting settled, I lost ten pounds that first month with no effort at all.

After the stove was delivered, the maid spent an entire day trying to get it cleaned. Whenever we moved and returned military appliances, they had to be spotless. Evidently, this was not the case in Turkey. She worked and sweated, mumbled under her breath, and finally declared it good enough for me to cook dinner. We plugged it in and turned on a burner. Nothing happened! She looked at me; I looked at her; we both wanted to cry. I felt frustrated and very sorry for her, but she recovered and went home. The next day Frank got the base to send someone over to check out the stove's problem. The repairman arrived at the arranged time, puttered around with the stove, and declared the stove broken and unfixable! They gave us a date for a new stove to be delivered. And so we continued to eat our meals out. A new stove was delivered, and that one was relatively clean. Our maid cleaned it in about an hour. We plugged it in, turned on a burner, and both of us broke into big smiles. It worked! I could finally cook a meal at home.

The next obstacle was the washer and dryer. We bought them from the military store, had them delivered, and got ready to wash a load of clothes. The washer wouldn't turn on. The store brought us a new one, and it worked. We put the wet clothes into the dryer and turned the dryer on. It started its cycle and immediately fast-forwarded to the end of the cycle. We didn't know what had happened. It refused to restart. Frank called the store. A repairman came out to fix our brand-new dryer. He announced it broken and unfixable. They delivered a new one. We put the wet clothes into the new dryer, and it fast-forwarded to the end of the cycle too! They came again; this time Frank and I were both out of control. We demanded to know why we kept getting lousy dryers. Were the companies sending defective machines to Turkey?

To make a long story shorter, someone finally checked the dryer's voltage. We had bought 220-volt appliances, but 110-volt dryers had been delivered, not once but twice. The third and last dryer worked.

Turkey is not the ideal situation for someone who has nothing to do to fill the spare time. Frank was interviewing at the high school and elementary school for a teaching position. Human resources decided he was not certified to teach anything. That was a great shock, because in Germany he was certified for just about everything. He gave up on human resources and went to see the high school principal, carrying his transcripts from the Air Force Academy, showing the credits for an engineering degree, his USC transcript showing a business degree, and Boston University transcript showing a master's in counseling, plus another extra thirty credits in counseling. The high school principal hired him almost on the spot to teach math. The principal did call human resources to see why they thought he wasn't certified. The answer was not forthcoming, and Frank was hired.

We had been in country three weeks. Now we had a working kitchen, a cool apartment, soil and flowers in the planters, ceiling fans with lights, a shiny marble floor, a working washer and dryer, and a maid to take care of the animals. We were also bug

Rose Porter

free once the screens were finally finished on all the windows, upstairs and down, and the balconies. Our home was safe from intruders due to our new wrought-iron security door. We both had teaching positions. We thought we were finally ready to start school. We decided to have a party and celebrate. One of my friends from Ramstein stated that only the Porters would have a party to celebrate the arrival of a washer and dryer! You had to be there, I guess, to understand our jubilation over something so commonplace and trivial as appliances. It's not something you had to worry about if you were stationed in Europe or the States.

School started. Kids arrived, ready to meet their new teachers and to see old friends. Everything was running smoothly. Because of the extremely hot temperatures, school started very early in the morning and was dismissed very early in the afternoon. The hottest time of the day was free for kids and teachers. About the third or fourth day of school, the elementary school's air conditioning quit. It was 110 F in the shade, no cool air anywhere. Windows were open, fans were blowing, and we were totally miserable. It was hard to even breathe, but we had to stay in school. We muddled through, kids and adults alike. None of us had the energy to do much, so we did what we could. The blessed weekend came, and a miracle occurred. The base engineers received the new parts and fixed the air conditioner. Life resumed on Monday amid smiling parents, children, and teachers!

A new crisis arrived early in September. When the hot temperatures eased, we were able to open the many windows for fresh air. Fresh air meant lots of dust flew into the apartment. Our maid was cleaning the floors daily to keep the dirt to a minimum. We came home from school one day to find straw from the broom decorating the kitchen sink. We realized that our maid was pouring the dirty floor water down the drain.

Since we weren't around to supervise her cleaning habits, we decided to have a garbage disposal installed. We ordered it from Istanbul and waited for its arrival; the store set up the installation for us. The installation date arrived, but the serviceman didn't. A new date was set. One man arrived, looked over the kitchen sink, and said he didn't have the tools or parts he needed. He left. The next day he returned with an English speaker; the two of them set to work. They took the sink apart and tried to explain the newest problem with our sink. They failed. The next day, three guys came; the newest serviceman was supposed to be a better English speaker who could explain the newest obstacle. It turned out we had a beautiful disposal, but an ugly sink! We needed to enlarge the cabinet and put in a much larger two-bowl model. We agreed, and five days later we had a magnificent sink. The newest sink cost us lots of money, but we had to admit that the sink and cabinet were, indeed, magnificent.

Our next problem with the maid came the day I asked her to wash the dirty lace curtains. If the windows were open, then the lace and privacy curtains became filthy. I assumed she knew how to wash them; after all, they were Turkish curtains! Well, she decided to wash all the lace curtains in one load. There were twelve windows on the first floor and twelve windows on the second floor.

All twenty-four floor-length lace curtains were in the washer. She'd decided to wash the lace ones first and to save the heavier privacy curtains for last. The washer filled with water, tried to agitate the heavy load, and died! We came home to find we no longer had a working washing machine, and we'd just celebrated its existence! The store was kind enough to replace it when their repairman couldn't fix the burned-out motor. We began to wonder why everyone else seemed to have maids who knew their jobs so well, when ours evidently didn't.

Next came the phone problem. It had taken us two or three trips to the phone company just to get the phone installed. We called home regularly, and it took an act of Congress to get through to the States. One night we were on the phone, talking to a friend in Destin, when the phone went dead. We tried to call again. No luck. Our phone was no longer working. That meant another trip to the phone company. The man on duty checked our phone line and told us the phone had been turned off due to an unpaid bill. We asked to see the bill, which had not been mailed to us. The bill, converted to dollars, was for $2.38. We paid the piddly sum in Turkish lira and asked that the phone be turned back on. He complained that Americans made too many phone calls to the States, and it was too expensive! We offered to pay a lump sum in advance, with the stipulation the company tell us when we needed to pay more instead of just turning our phone off. In Turkey, the phone is the only way the school or base officials could reach us in the event of a crisis. We didn't want to be stranded out in the suburbs without a way to communicate with the American government!

Then the soccer games started. Turks love their soccer! Whenever the Turkish team won, you would hear it, loud and clear. They piled into big farm trucks, standing room only, and drove around town shooting off their pistols. When you heard them, you had to immediately move indoors. People had been shot accidentally by these soccer lovers. They were shooting up into the air, but what goes up, must come down. Neither of us wanted to die in Turkey, and I definitely didn't want to visit a Turkish hospital.

About that time we got a message from the passport office that we needed to fly out of Turkey and reenter again so that we could get a visa. It seems many new people coming in had to follow this crazy procedure. We never did understand how we were allowed into the country in the first place if we'd needed a visa. We booked, at our own expense, a short tour of the Greek half of Cyprus. We flew over on a Friday night, stayed long enough to eat some Greek food and visit the museum, and we flew back into the Adana Airport on Sunday. We got our passports stamped and a visa, and we were finally legal. We never fully understood the reasoning behind our having to pay for the trip to get the visa; it was just another lack of communication between the human resources office and its teachers.

Hot weather turned cooler, and we started turning the heater on. We had a gas fireplace we wanted to use, so we had fuel delivered. Before we had a chance to light the fireplace, we discovered the fuel tank was leaking fuel. The landlord sent someone to fix it. The repairman put a can under the drip and told us it was ready for use. Consequently, we never used our brand-new fireplace during the two years we lived in Adana.

Turkey was certainly an exciting place to be in the 90's. School started earlier and got out early due to the hot weather. Since our part of town was the new part, building would take place during the night. The electric company would turn off the electricity to the apartment buildings and turn it back on again right before people were getting ready for work. The same happened with the water company. There were many mornings when our wind up alarm would go off but the heater or air conditioner was still off.

We'd go back to sleep and wait until we heard the *White* heater/air conditioner click on. Then it was time to get up and rush to shower and get to school before we were late.

After one of our nights with no water and electricity, we headed to school about 30 minutes later than usual. That was the same day the children's school bus passed a Turkish military bus which had been shot up by terrorists. Thankfully, their school bus had been en route about 30 minutes behind the Turkish bus so they didn't witness the attack.

We had been planning a trip to Damascus with our assistant principal. Damascus is the oldest city in the world and I wanted to visit it. Frank, being the retired military person, was hesitant but got a visa too. We were planning to ride the local bus and return by local bus. We had it all planned, but it was cancelled due to circumstances beyond our control.

About once a month we'd need a reality check so we'd go to the Hilton Hotel in Mersin. The Hilton allowed us to bring both dogs and both cats. The dogs loved the Hilton; they weren't allowed in the bar or dining room with us, but we took them everywhere else. The cats hated the Hilton, but then cats usually do hate new places. They stayed under the bed the whole two or three days we were there.

Our obnoxious cat didn't like the apartment either. In Germany she was allowed outside but not in Turkey. She decided she'd pay us back for bringing her to such a rotten place; she chewed the cables to my computer until it quit working. She always did it while we were gone so I had no idea what was happening until my computer died. I couldn't get replacements in Adana so I had to wait until Christmas. We went home for the break and stocked up on all the items we couldn't find in Turkey. That was lovingly called "visiting the big BX in the sky." American malls are wonderful places to stock up on essentials when you're living in a third-world country where the local military store is not as well stocked as others in larger bases around the world.

One of our favorite places to eat in Adana was an open air restaurant. They had the best pilic shish and sheperd's salad in town. The *Efes* beer wasn't too bad either. During the summer they would have tables set up on the sidewalk to offer ice cold watermelon and cold beer to the shoppers trying to get home. During the winter they hung blankets and heavy carpets to keep out the wind and cold. The inside would be hot from the heaters they kept around the eating area. It was great fun.

The best baked chicken came from the *Obalar* in the old market. My assistant principal took us there when we first arrived. It was awesome chicken with all the Turkish condiments included. The baked bananas were to die for. The only problem with the restaurant was the bathroom. I was told to never go to the ladies room. The men's room was almost too much for my boss.

If you wanted European food, then it was the *Pegasus*. They served the best cordon bleu in Adana and probably the only cordon bleu in town. It came with a real baked potato with all the trimmings and a great salad, not the usual shepherd's salad. It was a more expensive meal than we were used to ordering but who cares when you're homesick for some good German food.

The trip to Damascus was a bust but one Saturday we drove to Antioch. We saw the first church which was really just a cave but all around the church/cave were goats. The joke is goats have one leg longer than the other. That's how they manage to climb the rocky hills. We saw many black baby goats and fewer white ones.

Brass angels are one of the many things to buy in Turkey. Americans buy them in all the various heights so that they can be placed on the stairs of the house during the Christmas season. They are beautiful but brass does need to be polished. One of our Ramstein friends wanted an angel the height of her husband. One of our mutual friends managed to order one and get it finished in time to ship it for Christmas. The brass angel maker had to work feverishly because the first 2 or 3 did not turn out. He finally finished the one which passed inspection for mailing. It came in parts so that the angel could be mailed in several boxes. Our Ramstein friend was ecstatic when she saw her husband's angel. He was not as smitten as she was. But it made for a good joke, albeit an expensive one. Years later I learned they'd put the angel out on the street to get rid of it! I was so upset. I loved that angel and would have paid a lot of money for it if I'd only known. Really, how many people have a human sized angel on display in their house?

✤ C H A P T E R 2 9 ✤
Year 2: Adana

THE SECOND YEAR A TEACHER WAS ALMOST SHOT BY A TURKISH POLICEMAN. WE HAD been told to head for the base if we were involved in an accident with another car, bus, or bicycle, or if we killed an animal used for food. It was not unusual to see chickens or a loose cow on the highway while driving to base. The military would put us on the next flight out of Turkey. Someone else would be assigned to pack out your apartment and ship your car. Nobody wants to be put into a Turkish prison and that was the ultimate result if the Turkish cops got to you first.

The teacher was driving home from school after sunset. The cops wanted to pull her over for a standard check. It was dark; she was tired and couldn't see very well. She wasn't sure who was signaling her to pull over so she kept going. The cop shot at the fleeing car our teacher was driving. Once the light bulb had turned on and she realized she was hearing live ammo, she pulled over. She was taken to the Turkish police station; somehow the base found out about the shooting and a military police car went to rescue her. That incident caused quite a ruckus around school.

The second year the plumbing in the elementary school decided to break down. Since the kids couldn't flush, it was considered a health hazard. School was closed until the civil engineers could get the problem fixed. Air conditioning wasn't a health problem, but nonflushing toilets were. I got it. It made perfectly good sense to some people. But I still thought the base commander could have considered stifling heat a health hazard and closed the school the year before until the air conditioner could be fixed.

For the Thanksgiving break we flew to Izmir to meet some friends from Boise. They enjoyed a van tour of Efes while we shopped at Roza's Carpets and Hanefe's gold store. We stayed at the Hilton Hotel where we got a military discount and the hotel had an armed guard to check people going in and out of the hotel or its shops. The top floor had a bar and restaurant that gave us a great view of the city lights and the Mediterranean.

At Christmas we flew home to see friends and relatives. It took us twenty-four hours to travel from our front door in Adana to our front door in Tampa. We had to make that trip several times during our two-year tour due to family illnesses. Flights leaving Turkey and Frankfurt leave on time; it was the flights in the States that were the problem. Delays due to weather and cancellations would probably make the journey even longer nowadays. The only time we were late taking off from Frankfurt was due to ice on the wings which had to be corrected before we could depart.

In May we rented a Turkish car to visit Nemrut Dagi which is in PKK territory belonging to the Kurdish people of Turkey. Nemrut Dagi is a seven-thousand-foot mountain of rocks that is the burial place for King Antiochos who considered himself important enough to have that honor. He thought he was a god and entitled to this outlandish burial site! Statues of Antiochos and the gods were at the top of the mountain.

The PKK was a terrorist group that controlled the area we needed to journey through. They were fighting the Turkish government which meant the Turkish military. Americans were discouraged by the military to go sightseeing there. We didn't want to drive our car with a plate that identified us as Americans.

The rock pyramid could be seen from twenty miles away. We were told the only way to get there was by car. There were many roadblocks on the route, where Turkish military or Turkish police checked cars. We drove slowly and carefully through all the roadblocks. If we were stopped, they immediately let us continue when they discovered we were Americans. They loved us!

We arrived at the closest town to the burial site and checked into the only hotel. We hadn't made reservations. After all, who drives through PKK country? The kilim on the floor was threadbare and faded but still being used; we started to believe those sales pitches about the rugs and kilims that would last forever. We ate dinner in the hotel; neither of us can remember what we had besides beer. Neither one of us got sick from it. That was the good news. The bedsprings were noisy, the mattress was lumpy, the towels were as threadbare as the kilims downstairs in the lobby, and the shower was cold—no stars for that hotel!

Bright and early the next morning we started driving. All we had to do was focus on the pyramid; we couldn't get lost. The roads were bad, and the trip took us longer than expected. As we approached the hill, we decided to stop at a small cafe at the bottom. There were lots of men sitting around under the trees drinking beer and talking. We sat down, ordered beer, and were soon joined by some of the men. They were interested in who we were and why we were in the area. Frank gave them a long-winded history lesson on the pyramid and why we wanted to visit the area—which they bought! They then identified themselves as being members of the PKK. They gave us hints on the best way to get to the top, where to park the car, and the easiest route for the final ten-minute hike to the top. We thanked them, got back in the car, and breathed an enormous sigh of relief. We took off and never looked back.

The worst part of the climb was the final ten-minute hike. The stones became smaller and smaller; the smaller they got, the more they slipped and slid. You'd take two steps and slide back three but we finally made it to the top. We were astounded to see a helipad. We could have come in a helicopter and saved ourselves the long drive, the really bad hotel, and the unmemorable dinner. We would have missed seeing the

Rose Porter

PKK too. When we related this story to our American military friend, he reminded us that helicopters make a really good target for the PKK to shoot down. I guess driving was the only option after all.

After shopping in Izmir, Turkey, the rest of the world is second rate. The city continues to be our favorite. You can buy anything there. We even had the brass decoration on our English brass bed repaired. It had been damaged in the move, so we took the pieces to our gold merchant, and he sent a young Turkish boy with us to the right repair shop. In two days our bed was repaired like new, at a price we'd never see again once we left the country.

During those days, I added to the copper collection I'd started on my first trip to Athens almost twenty years before. There are lots of copper merchants, and all are willing to sell you your heart's desire. If you want a set of cooking pots lined with tin or canisters, lunchboxes, or large planters, you can find them in Izmir's bazaar area. When you buy certain copper pieces, the merchant will offer to stamp the bottom with the sultan's crest; all they asked of us was to pick out which sultan's stamp we desired The stamp made the piece of copper an antique and much more valuable. Turkey and Korea are the only two countries, in my experience, where you can get ready-made antiques on the spot.

After two years, we left Turkey to return to the States. Getting out of Turkey was almost as bad as getting into it and getting settled. When we'd gotten married, I'd gone to a hyphened name. Entering Turkey was a real treat for me because I had to sign my very long last name about fifty times. I swore when we got to a new country, I was dropping my maiden name. Also, whatever you bring into Turkey, you must take out with you. If your toaster died, you took it to your next country with you. If your TV died, it had to leave with you. The local joke around the base was if your car died in Turkey, you had to put it on a ferry and dump it in the Med to remove it from your paperwork. We never had to cross that bridge so who knows the real answer to having a car die in Turkey? The Turkish Customs officials checked and double-checked all our paperwork; since I'd signed my name fifty times coming in, I had to sign it fifty times again going out.

Moving to Turkey was quite an ordeal. We're glad we got to live there, but we've decided it was much more fun to just visit. All you need is a visa which you can buy at the airport.

❧ CHAPTER 30 ❧
1995–2001
Tampa, Florida

AFTER TWO YEARS IN TURKEY, WE MOVED BACK HOME TO TAMPA. MY NINETY-PLUS-year old mother moved in with us and we settled down to life in America. We had both lived more of our adult lives overseas than at home. We went through culture shock again. We didn't know anything about cell phones, phone contracts, or which phone company was the best and cheapest.

Frank went to a middle school to inquire about a job opening and was hired on the spot—the same man who had been told he wasn't certified to teach anything in Turkey! I called an old friend and learned she had become a principal. Between her and my old principal, now in human resources, I returned to my old school.

Several incidents happened while we were teaching in Tampa. After my first year back, I ended up teaching at one of the oldest and worst-located schools in the city. We had our own cop who enforced the appropriate behavior of students. Sometimes you'd see a police car arrive and leave with an older kid who'd brought a gun or knife to school. That was almost normal for the school which was in a beautiful old two-story red-brick building.

School started earlier than most elementary schools but ended earlier too. The neighborhood was poor with lots of welfare families and drugs prevailed. Two buses picked up kids from the outskirts of the school's district. The rest walked or were picked up in grand cars by a parent. Once a parent arrived with her pet snake curled around her neck; I still shudder when I remember her. Our principal was alerted, and she immediately sent the cop over to keep her away from the buses and the school. She complied, picked up her kid, and walked home!

If we wanted a parent conference, we'd drive to the family's house and knock on the door; if you sent a note saying you were coming, nobody would be home. If you asked a parent to come to school for a conference, no one showed up. It was that kind of neighborhood. We even had an open house at the local meeting hall but very few parents came to talk to their kids' teachers.

My favorite home visit was made to discuss reading practice at home, the usual teacher request: read with your kid each night. A new Cadillac was parked in front of the home so I knew someone was there. When I knocked, the father was gracious and invited me in. The ramshackle shack, as seen from the outside, was a magazine advertisement on the inside: leather furniture, an oriental rug on the floor, nice drapes, an expensive dining room set, and so forth. Amazing! He must have had a great job; doing what is up to your imagination.

Later I taught in a gated community in New Tampa. New Tampa is the new construction located outside of the city close to the swamps that inhabit Florida. A six-foot wire fence surrounded the school playground. One morning we were told over the intercom that specials had been canceled for the time being and to stay inside our classrooms. Later we were informed that a six-foot alligator had been seen going over the playground fence! Animal Control had been called but couldn't find the alligator when they arrived. Evidently he had left the same way he arrived; if you've never seen an alligator go over a tall fence, it's amazing. They sort of slide up and over.

Another incident was published in the city's newspaper. K-mart had been closed to customers because a huge rattlesnake had been found curled up on one of the shelves in the back. Animal Control was called and took the rattlesnake away after checking for babies.

If you're a golfer and move to Tampa, beware of lightning. Golfers are struck by lightning more in Tampa than other cities which has earned Tampa the not-so-nice title of Lightning Capital of the World. It can be a sunny day with not one cloud in the sky, and then first comes the lightning, then the thunder. It's scary, to say the least.

We still had both cats with us. The obnoxious one liked to hunt for snakes to bring inside and dump in our bed while we were still in it. The first time she did it, we both jumped out of bed thinking it was a coral snake. It certainly looked like one. We did some research and found out it was a harmless ring neck. The second time she delivered one to our bed, Frank calmly carried it outside with the barbecue tongs and tossed it over our back fence. We figured our neighbor's cat could play with it for a while.

Frank got up one Sunday afternoon to get a cold drink from the kitchen just in time to see a huge black snake getting ready to slide under our stove. He yelled for the obnoxious cat. Our great female hunter sank her teeth into the snake just as he was almost under the stove. Frank grabbed the tongs again and, with the help of a broom, carried the fat snake outside and threw him over our side fence. Later we discovered the black snake lived under the tall bush outside our next-door neighbor's front door. The snake had disappeared for a couple of days and his children were getting anxious! Evidently, the black snake had adopted the family, or the family had adopted him. Whichever it was, it didn't matter to us as long as we never saw the black snake again in our yard—or, even worse, inside the house!

The squirrel population in our area was out of control too. They loved to race across our pool cage and annoy the cats and dogs. The dogs would bark and chase them from one end of the cage to the other; the cats would jump up, trying to sink their teeth into one. The squirrels loved all the action! No way could the cats jump high enough to be a threat to them. My husband, however, was another story. He knew he was smarter than the squirrels, so he went to the hardware store and bought a hand-held trap for small animals. He baited the trap with peanut butter and started trapping the squirrels. We had an empty lot about four blocks away with a gigantic oak tree, complete with lots of moss hanging from it. He'd drive the angry squirrels over to the lot and release them near the tree. We probably relocated thirty squirrels to that empty lot! It became a lot more peaceful around our pool area.

We still spent our Christmas vacations traveling. Frank got to climb the Mayan pyramids in Mexico and compare them to the Egyptian construction. He liberated a few items from the local shops to add to his history collection for school, and I found some authentic onyx and lapis lazuli bracelets set in silver. The Mexican food was really different from the version you get in the States. Not only was it cheap, even in the four-star hotels, but it was truly an unforgettable experience. The food in our favorite Tex-Mex establishment in Tampa never tasted as good again. Shopping in Mexico City was good too. After we returned home, we learned from a jeweler at the mall that the Mexicans make a lot of synthetic stones. It's too bad we didn't talk to that jeweler before we went to Mexico!

Hong Kong was on our list to revisit one last time before the British lease ran out and it was reclaimed by China. We were able to make the trip at the last possible moment. China, one of the countries I couldn't visit from Korea, was just as I pictured it. It was so cold my toes stayed numb the entire ten days we toured: Beijing, the terracotta soldiers at Xian, and Guangzhou (Canton). Our hotel beds were stacked with blankets to keep us warm, along with the heaters on the walls, but my toes never warmed up. I took my heaviest coat, my hat, and my fur-lined boots, all from my life in Germany, but they were not enough to fight the chill of Beijing. Beijing was a large city, with lots of people riding bicycles and lots of people talking on cell phones. We'd only been back in the States two years, but it seemed as if the Chinese were more hooked on cells than Americans were.

The Forbidden City was a once-in-a- lifetime tour. My friend in Destin wanted a present from the city, so I bought her a jade necklace. Later she told me the necklace had broken during the middle of a student support group meeting, and beads had rolled all over the floor. The meeting immediately stopped. Everybody involved in the meeting got down on the floor and started picking up beads and searching the corners for more. Once they'd found all the obvious beads, the meeting continued. When the American jeweler restrung the beads, only four or five beads had been lost. The string the Chinese used originally wasn't very strong, so it's best to have pearls or other precious beads restrung by a professional when you return home. My pearls from Japan were restrung by Hanefe, our Turkish jeweler; he put individual knots between the pearls so that if the strand did break, potentially only one pearl would be lost.

After the Forbidden City and Tiananmen Square, we flew to Xian to see the tomb of First Emperor Shihuangdi. They built the museum around the excavation site of the terracotta soldiers and horses. The museum was just as cold inside as the outside temperature was.

There were miniature soldiers and horses for sale, and you could also have a full-size soldier shipped back to America. We were told that if the soldier broke during shipping, another one would be shipped. Sometimes it took three shipments before a soldier arrived in mint condition! After we returned to Florida and visited Epcot, we found miniature soldiers for sale in the stores there; they were cheaper that the ones we bought in Xian. Go figure. At least we know that ours really came from Xian.

The tour included a visit to the Great Wall; we took our obligatory walk and bought a T-shirt to prove it. It's the only thing I bought for myself, so when we got home, of course, I had to wear it. Then I had to wash it. True to third-world traditions, it shrank during washing and became too small to ever wear again. I took it to our local framers and had it framed. Now it hangs on a wall with the date of our trip permanently written on it. Every T-shirt I've ever bought in a third-world country has followed the same path—not being framed, but shrinking so small to be beyond wearing again.

We cruised down the Li River to Yangzhou, where we made a shopping trip through their market. Then back on the boat and onward to Guilin. There were only nineteen of us on the cruise. Only three of us did not eat lunch on the boat. As we'd leisurely floated downstream, we all saw the workers wash the food in the river. The dirty dishes were washed in the river. The water they cooked with came from the river. And so forth and so on … until lunch was served. The other sixteen ate the delicious-smelling authentic Chinese dishes, and all sixteen of them became painfully ill about two hours later. All of us except for the medical person got ill at least once before we returned to the States; she didn't because of all the homeopathic herbs and medicines she'd started taking two weeks before leaving the States.

As we flew south toward Hong Kong, conditions warmed us up considerably. The food was better, the people friendlier, and the hotels were larger. Canton was delightful. The people were beautiful, and the weather was finally sunny and warm. We spent one day and night touring the city, complete with a visit to a medical school for an acupuncture demonstration, and then we departed by train for Hong Kong.

Hong Kong had not changed very much since the last time we'd visited. The airport was new and out of the city. The Peninsular Hotel on the Kowloon side was still the place to go for High Tea. The little boys in their uniforms still walked around looking for individuals who'd received phone calls. The New Year's Day Buffet was worth the money to shellfish lovers. The buffet's worth the money even if you're allergic to shellfish and have to settle for meat!

We went back to Jimmy's Kitchen for dinner. Jimmy served cordon bleu with baked potatoes and a great salad. The prices seemed to have doubled in the ten plus years since we'd had reservations. Food in Hong Kong isn't cheap to begin with. The Hard Rock Cafe was still on Hong Kong Island, so we had to take the ferry across if we wanted to visit.

We flew out a couple of days earlier than the rest of the tour so that we could spend some time in Honolulu. It was windy and cool enough for my heavy coat. I was surprised to say the least, but it was sunny. All my prior visits had been during warmer seasons.

I'd never go back to China in December again. I read all the Pearl S. Buck books during my early school days, and I'd always wanted to visit Shanghai. One of these days, I still might.

Another Christmas vacation was spent in South America. We walked on Copacabana Beach, in Rio de Janeiro, and visited the massive statue of Christ the Redeemer on top of Corcovado mountain. I don't remember any funny stories in South America except for Rio. We went to the Stern Jewelry store and asked to see amethyst necklaces. A woman I can only describe as a Nazi came to wait on us. She looked, walked, and acted like my worst nightmare. She snubbed her nose because we didn't want to spend $7,000 for the stone she'd brought. Another guy came over and introduced himself as Turkish. We discussed Turkey for a few minutes and he was very pleased to help us. Frank made a drawing for him and the amethyst necklace was delivered to our hotel the next afternoon. It was beautifully handcrafted and very reasonably priced.

Buenos Aires was just another big city like Paris. We went to a gaucho ranch, where Frank and others rode the Argentinean horses; later we were served a typical Argentinean barbecue; the beef was too tough for me. By the way, that was our Christmas dinner. I like our American barbecues much better. We walked the square featured in the movie *Evita*, with Madonna and Antonio Banderas. We visited the Hard Rock Cafe and discovered all Hard Rocks do not cook food the same way. The salads are the only item we've found that is essentially prepared and looks the same in all the Cafes we've visited around the world. And we have the T-shirts to prove we visited them.

Santiago, Chile was our next stop. We didn't spend too long there but long enough for breakfast and poached eggs. I hadn't had poached eggs since the Oriental Hotel in Bangkok. They brought back pleasant memories.

Flying to Lima, Peru, was a pleasant trip that ended at a comfortable hotel out of the city. The temperatures were pleasant and the pool looked inviting. Lima was crowded. The downtown apartments and balconies looked a lot like buildings we'd seen in Spain. We met a local art salesman the first time we got off the tour bus to check out the local sight. He kept trying to get us to buy an ugly green picture of the ruins at Machu Picchu. We kept saying no. When we got off the bus at the next stop on the tour, the same man continued to try to sell us the same painting. After about the fourth time, we bought the ugly painting just to get rid of him. Once we got it home, I took it to our local framer and had it framed. Now that it's framed, it's a masterpiece! It's amazing what a frame does for a watercolor. It's beautiful and hangs proudly in our stairwell.

The only food I remember from Lima was a tuna sandwich we ordered while we were waiting to continue our journey to Cusco and Machu Picchu. Imagine if you will two pieces of bread, topped with the tuna fish the cook took out of a can after draining the oil from it. Now cut that sandwich in half and add greasy potato chips. The final straw was the bill we got—just under twenty dollars for two sandwiches and two beers (remember this was 1999). Meals like that make you want to snap your fingers and to suddenly appear in an American *Village Inn Restaurant* so that you can order a real tuna sandwich.

After Lima we flew to Cusco, a beautiful little town. It was at such high elevation that we had to drink a special concoction so we didn't pass out when we stood up. We took a train the next day to Machu Picchu, where my history-teacher husband was once again in heaven. After a day of exploring, we rode the train back down the mountain to Cusco, where we welcomed in the year 2000. We left very early the next morning for the trip back to Tampa and school. After we got home, *National Geographic* had an article on the Nazca Lines in Peru. The only way to really see them is from the air. Built in 800 BC, they're rock lines in the shape of monkeys, birds, and other animals. If only we'd known that prior to the trip, we could have booked a side trip to fly over them. It would be worth going back to Peru someday to see the Lines.

We took a three-country tour for the next Christmas vacation, starting with Spain's largest cities. Portugal was a new country for both of us. I doubt that we would have planned a trip there, but it was included on the Spain and Morocco trip. We flew into Madrid about eight in the morning, arriving after a night trying to sleep on the flight from Tampa. We were all shown to our rooms to wait for our city tour, which began around two that afternoon. Most of us used the time to sleep in a comfortable bed.

The Prada Museum was right down the street, and the Hard Rock Cafe was a ten-minute taxi ride in heavy traffic. We made it to both on our own. We loved the wide, tree-covered sidewalks, and we sampled our first tapas in the local bar. The weather was pleasant which made walking about the city pleasurable.

We continued via bus the next morning to our next stop; we traveled to Seville, Cordoba, Granada and the Alhambra, and Valencia before driving into Lisbon and then on to Fatima, Portugal.

After leaving Rota, we drove to Gibraltar and crossed on the ferry to Tangiers. We kept driving through the mountains, past towns still inhabited by French, to Marrakesh and back to Tangiers, stopping in Casablanca, home of Humphrey Bogart and Ingrid Bergman's movie of the same name and Harry's Bar. The bar, in a four-star hotel was being renovated, so we had to view it from the hall. But an American lady has since opened a restaurant called Harry's Cafe to commemorate the movie. It stays open seven days a week for the tourists.

We continued to Rabat, which is a great city, and finally went back to Tangiers where we spent one night. Marrakesh was our favorite city with its snake charmers and open-air markets; Tangiers was our least-favorite city. In Tangiers a group of women accosted us, hitting me on the back and shoulders because I wouldn't buy their trinkets. You have to remember that the Moroccan people are very poor, and selling junk to tourists is the only way some of them can provide for their families. Frank came to my rescue and we left the area without any more problems.

I think our favorite summer trip might have been returning to Italy and Greece. The weather in southern Italy was warm when we landed in Rome but as we toured north to Venice, the weather grew chilly. I ended up buying a sweater the first night. After that Venice became more comfortable; the sights were astounding as they always are, and we enjoyed the "real" Italian food.

We took an overnight ferry to Greece, which has been our only cruise, if you can call an overnight ferry going on a cruise. It was just long enough for us. The food was tour food—not the best—but we were ready to revisit Sparta, Corinth, Delphi, and Athens. We finally made it to Santorini for the first, but not last, time. The history museum was closed for renovation, and I knew we'd have to return at another time so that my history-teacher husband could obtain firsthand knowledge of its contents for his high school students. Santorini is a romantic island. The biggest town is on top of the cliffs above the Aegean. Tourists can disembark from their cruise ships and choose to walk up the rocky path, ride a donkey up, or use the funicular. We flew in, so getting to the town was much easier. Shopping is plentiful for Greek jewelry, clothing, and paintings, as were the wonderful Greek restaurants. You can't get authentic Greek dishes else-where as good as those in Santorini.

Throughout all the years in Tampa, we found a new getaway from the day-to-day stress of teaching. Once a month, sometimes twice, we'd drive to Dade City, the city of my birth, and visit the *Williams Clothing Store* and their *Lunch on Limoges* restaurant. They sold clothing that the owners would buy in New York or Atlanta, wherever the big clothing warehouses had big sales, and sometimes jewelry from Europe or Asia was also offered. One of the owners had inherited the building from his family, and his partner was the chef. Together they ran the store and restaurant. They became our "boys" in Dade City; neither were boys, but rather middle-age men, but who cared?

After shopping, we would have a French lunch, of sorts. The food wasn't really French, but Limoges made you think of France. The food was more southern, and their desserts were a mix of different cultures. Frank's favorite was Pecan Chicken, which was written up in *Southern Living*; mine was the Grecian Grouper. Grouper is famous in Florida, but the sauce of tomatoes, spices, and black olives always reminded me of Greece. Our favorite cake was the Fairy Cake—a three-layer white cake with fresh strawberries and whipped cream between the layers and on top. Between the carrot muffins and the dessert, we always had to take some food home for dinner. Eating everything would definitely make you feel too full and out of sorts the rest of the afternoon.

After five years, my mother left us, and we reapplied for DoDDS. I was told by human resources that I couldn't expect to just go right back to Germany; I had to go to a less desirable location first. So I was offered a gifted position in Okinawa. I'd never been to Okinawa, but I was willing to go anywhere to get back to Europe. We had traveled to Tokyo but only long enough to ride the bullet train and to see the cherry blossoms. Tokyo had been fun, so I signed on the dotted line, and we started planning our departure for Okinawa.

We had to sell the house, arrange plane reservations, put our wonderful Camry in storage for nine months, and get the furniture packed up to leave. We put most of the furniture and the winter clothes into storage; our household goods for Okinawa were limited to mostly summer clothes and one coat. We decided to take only the oldest of the old furniture.

Frank put up a FOR SALE BY OWNER sign and sold the house to the first person who rang the doorbell. He and the older gentlemen shook hands on the deal; no money was exchanged, and no agreement to buy was signed. This might sound strange to people who know me, but I knew something Frank didn't know. The man was the grandfather of a student from my latest school which was right down the street. He had a reputation as being richer than most of the local residents of the golfing community and had lots of property, including a house on the beach in Clearwater. I knew he was good for the money.

And, true to his word, after we'd all arrived at the lawyer's office at the appointed time and signed the paperwork, we received our money in *cash* and immediately drove to the bank to deposit it. The next day we boarded our plane and started our journey to Japan. We carried Patches, the cat, along with two large suitcases, which would tide us over until our air shipment of clothing arrived. We had started another adventure!

CHAPTER 31

2001–2002
Okinawa

AFTER RUSHING TO PACK OUR POSSESSIONS AND TO TURN OVER OUR HOUSE KEYS TO the new owner, we arrived in Okinawa, Japan, just a couple of days before school started. We had the German farm cat with us; the other three pets had gone on to kitty and doggy heaven by then. A volunteer teacher met us at the airport, took us to a hotel, and dumped us at the door. We were more than surprised, but we shrugged it off. After all, we had been around the world at least twice by then, so we could find the hotel manager without too much help.

The hotel did not have any stars. It ranks among the worst hotels I've ever stayed in. The bathtub was straight out of my first trip to Athens. It was a half-bath, or to explain it another way, it had a seat and a basin for your feet; it had two levels. You sat in the tub, but your feet rested on the lower level.

The first night in country we felt earthquake tremors; that weekend there were typhoon warnings! Welcome to Okinawa.

No dining room or attendant or manager appeared the next morning, so we contemplated our fate. Did we hang around to see if someone was coming to get us? Did we call a taxi? We couldn't find a phone or anyone to give us a number to call, so we decided to start walking. How hard could it be to find the marine base where I was assigned? Our hotel was in a hilly area, so walking downhill was easy. When we made it down to the level area, we found a taxi and asked to be taken to the marine base.

He obliged and dropped us off in front of the school's office; from there the assistant principal drove us to another base where human resources was located. We had to fill out more paperwork. Nothing had changed since we'd left Turkey; the DoDDS world still revolved on paperwork.

The greatest thing about our hotel's location was a really awesome Japanese restaurant was close by; our first meal was totally out of this world—fresh, raw fish! I have no idea what kind of fish it was, but I was in love with the food; my husband would have preferred steak tartare. Living in Japan would prove to be another adventure in food.

We took a taxi to the used-car lots and bought two cars right away both with right hand drive. The most expensive one was just under $5,000; the second one was $3,700. They were both great cars. We sold them for the buying price when we left. We never had any problems with them even though we'd never heard of the models before. Lots of Japanese models are never exported.

Frank got a teaching position and we moved to another hotel close to Kadena AFB. This hotel was newer, larger, and appeared cleaner than our previous one. During typhoons life off-base went on as usual. We were able to drive to restaurants for meals. We were in the middle of a strong typhoon when 9-11 happened. We had gotten up in the middle of the night and turned on the TV to see what the typhoon was doing. We watched 9-11 instead. Both the air force and the marines had real bullets in their rifles the very next day. School was closed for a short while because all the bases were on alert. If no one knew for sure whether the rifles were loaded with live ammo before, there was no doubt in anyone's mind after 9-11. That fact was widely advertised throughout the bases and the local shopping community. The Okinawans had been alerted to stay calm.

After about a month in hotels, we moved on base for the first and only time in our careers overseas. The concrete-block townhouse, valued at $55,000, was perfect for us. Two bedrooms, one bath, living room, dining room, kitchen, and one driveway. I was responsible for not destroying the house and had to sign a statement, acknowledging the cost of the apartment if we burned it down or damaged it in any way. Once we moved on base we were under the control of the military. During a typhoon, the base had stringent rules for people living on base. We had to stay inside, even if the eye was over the base. There was no grilling on the patio even if the sun was shining. The restaurants and other facilities were closed. But living on base allowed you to listen to the local traffic off base; life proceeded as usual for the Okinawans.

We socialized with the teachers and I started a dining-out activity once or twice a month. Okinawa City has lots of garlic restaurants and lots of chicken restaurants along with the usual seafood places. Kadena had some good restaurants along with the usual food courts.

In November I attended a workshop in Tokyo held in the military hotel; food was served to our group in one of the private dining rooms. We were at lunch the first day, doing what elementary teachers are famous for when they get together—talking about school! I looked across the rather large round table at a familiar face; I could not for the life of me recall her name or where I knew her from. Suddenly, the light bulb came on; she was one of my friends from Newfoundland! I hadn't seen her since 1973, almost thirty years before. I had tried to find her on my first trip to Hawaii, but her Japanese name is as common as Smith or Jones are in America. One of her habits in Newfoundland was to trim the crust off her toast in the morning; it was her way of dieting, since all the calories are in the crust. She was still practicing the habit in Tokyo. We had a private gossip fest later about all the "old-timers" we'd left behind in the frozen wilderness of the north.

We were planning trips to Australia, New Zealand, and India when my transfer to Germany was announced. I was shocked! I had applied but had never dreamed I would get it after only nine months on the island. People were upset with me; some had been asking for transfers for years and years. However, they had requested specific schools and certain grade levels. I said I'd go anywhere in Germany and teach anything I was certified for. Being willing to take potluck usually works. Earthquake tremors and typhoon warnings accompanied our last weekend in Okinawa.

❧ C H A P T E R   3 2 ❧
Moving to Mannheim

WE WERE TRAVELING WITH PATCHES AND PLANNED TO DELAY OUR TRAVEL TO ENJOY a few days in Honolulu; we knew we'd have to put the cat in quarantine. He would not be a happy camper. The quarantine officials met us and took Patches away with them for his vacation. We checked in at the Hale Koa to spend some time on Waikiki Beach and relax in the city where we'd been married twenty-one years earlier. About four days into our stay, we decided to rent a car and check on Patches. He'd never been in quarantine before, but we knew he'd hate being separated from us or the other animals in the kennel. It was just as we had thought; he turned his back to us and ignored us, so we left. Cats! Dogs are such good kissers.

We flew from Honolulu to New York City to enjoy the Fourth of July with some great fireworks. I'd made reservations at a Manhattan hotel that would allow Patches to stay with us. We had no problems at the hotel. The Fourth of July fireworks were awesome to behold.

We left New York City and flew to Destin to spend some time visiting old friends from Ramstein and Turkey. When it came time to leave, we arrived at the Fort Walton Beach Airport with all the paperwork for Patches. We checked in and started through passport control with him in his carrier. It was too hot to let him wait with the luggage to be put on the plane. Then our problems began.

The security team wanted to send him through the x-ray machine. We very politely but firmly said no. Then they decided we had to take him out of the cage so that they could wand him. Evidently, cats can have explosive devices hidden somewhere under their fur. We tried to say no again but to no avail. The most wonderful cat in the world (and clawless) was picked up by the passport control official and held while his partner used the wand on him. Talk about insanity! The poor cat had been a model traveler until that happened. At that point, he couldn't control himself anymore and started wailing pitifully which made every passenger in the terminal turn around to see what was happening. Then his legs began to twist and turn, and his clawless paws accidentally hit one of the men. The man thought the cat was going to scratch his eyes out and almost dropped him. Frank and I were beside ourselves and helped the gentlemen put Patches back into his cage. The men, now embarrassed and unhappy to have been a part of the drama, rushed us through the checkpoint. The crowd was beside itself, as were we!

Patches settled down once he was safely back in familiar territory. Frank carried him outside to the steps where a different agent put him into the air-conditioned airplane.

We flew on to Washington, DC, where we needed to visit the American Embassy. Frank had written the Hilton and asked if we could stay there; he explained that this particular cat had been welcomed in other Hilton Hotels around the world with no problems. The Hilton wrote back that, of course, Patches was more than welcome to stay at their hotel since he was a seasoned Hilton visitor! And, that's the story of why we love Hilton Hotels.

❧ CHAPTER 33 ❧
2002–2005
Mannheim, Germany

WE ARRIVED IN MANNHEIM IN EARLY AUGUST TO START THE PROCESS ALL OVER again. New house, new curtains, getting furniture delivered, buying cars, and so forth. Frank taught at the middle school teaching math, and I was at the elementary school teaching fifth grade.

Our most interesting story was spring break in Jordan. We spent a day exploring Petra which is well worth a trip if you are in the area. The movie *Indiana Jones and the Last Crusade* with Harrison Ford and Sean Connery was filmed at the site. One of the local guides asked us if we were there to pay Jordan for the filming rights. The local joke was that Steven Spielberg and George Lucas never paid Jordan for the privilege of filming in Petra so the tourists needed to do so for them.

While shopping around Amman, we noticed lots of tours to Israel. Turns out it was much easier to get in and out of Israel from Jordan. It eliminated all the hassles by the passport officials in Tel Aviv. We contacted an Israeli tour guide who agreed to pick us up at the border early in the morning and return us to the border with Jordan that same night. We hired a driver to take us to the border, walked through passport control, and met our waiting guide. He looked like my mental image of a TV version of a Mossad agent—good-looking enough to challenge James Bond, any of the James Bonds!

We arrived in Jerusalem around ten in the morning on Good Friday. As we were walking to the Church of the Holy Sepulcher, Frank felt someone trying to pick his pocket. When he turned around, he saw a man in a priest's robe. Frank was too fast for the thief but it was a good wakeup call.

We visited leather shops, the spice market, and the Jewish Quarter before we started back late in the afternoon. The Jewish Quarter is a large group of shops where tourists are welcome to spend their money. It provides the best shopping anywhere for Roman glass jewelry. The Roman glass that is dug up around the excavations is then made into jewelry with stamped silver. Prices are reasonable. It was a great trip. We revisited one of our favorite cities and enjoyed some great Israeli food. There were no lines at passport control either way.

Mannheim was a great experience for the fifth graders. Our Host Nation teacher was an exceptional person. Every year for decades she'd organized a four-day overnight trip in May for the fifth graders who were graduating and moving on to the middle school. Every year in September, she'd remind the students, who really didn't need reminding, that we would all travel to a youth hostel near Cochem that spring. We would visit castles, hike through a natural-setting zoo, eat meals in the large dining room together, wash dishes, make beds, set tables, and so forth. The culminating trip was to Trier to tour the Roman baths and the city itself, as well as visit the weekly market.

In order to be invited, each student had to help raise the money to pay for the trip. Parents were only permitted to pay a small portion of the price. The students had to do the majority of the work. They hosted bake sales, sold dill pickles, washed cars, babysat, and did whatever else was necessary to raise money. If they got into trouble during the year, they stood to lose their invitation for the trip. It was also a great way to keep rowdy and hormone-stricken kids in line for nine months!

The teachers loved the trip too—no lesson plans to write, no homework to grade, just good, clean fun for four days. The students had German work to complete each day that included daily journals and completing fill-in-the-blank questions about the castles and fortresses. They had to listen carefully to the tour guides, who would provide the required answers. The work had to be turned in when we returned to school, and our Host Nation teacher graded the papers.

One teacher stayed behind at the elementary school with the students who did not attend. Only a few had to stay behind because of behavior. Some would PCS during that week; some came down with the flu or something medical at the last minute, and so forth. No one wanted to stay and do work while the majority were having four days of *fun*!

On one of our Christmas trips home to the States, Frank wanted to buy a miniature schnauzer puppy. We had lost Patches, the cat, days before we left due to liver complications. If we found a puppy, then we were also going to get a tabby cat so they'd grow up together and be friends. At least, that was our goal. Frank called around the state of Florida and found no puppy. But, nevertheless, he insisted that I get a kitten. I refused. No puppy, no kitten—that was the deal! Christmas morning I got up to find Frank surfing on the Internet, seeking a puppy. He was determined I was getting a kitten to replace Patches. A local family had just placed an advertisement for a female, more salt than pepper. We drove to their house. As their kid was opening presents, we bought a puppy. We took Misty home.

Then we began the search for a tabby about the same age. Destin has a Cattery, which we'd visited with Patches on prior trips, so we started there. No tabby kittens. I placed my order, and then we went home and called some vet clinics and the Humane Society. No luck. The next day Frank started calling the same people from the day before. "Has our order been delivered yet?" The answer was always the same—no.

Finally, one day he called and our order had just been filled by a lady with too many animals. We went to her house and listened to her tale of woe. It seemed the little malnourished kitten had struggled into her yard and up her steps to the front door. Her kids discovered it, and, of course, the kids wanted to keep it. Mom assumed the job of feeding it with an eye dropper, trying to keep it alive. She did a marvelous job, and the kitten took over the animals' bedroom. The family had three dogs that all slept together in the utility room at night. Well, TC, the tabby cat, climbed to the top of the heap! The family was becoming too attached to the kitten, and Mom really didn't want any more animals to feed, so she'd called the Cattery.

We paid Mom for the shots TC had gotten, and off we went to get the paperwork done for flying back to Germany. At that time, it was torture to take an animal to Germany—so many rules. Our flight was due to leave, and we were in danger of having to leave TC in Destin. We had to get special paperwork from the Department of Health in Gainesville; that took a few days. Finally, everything was ready, and we were off with "the twins."

All we had to do was manage to board the plane at the Fort Walton Beach Airport with both animals in tow. We weren't looking forward to it; we expected the worst, and we weren't disappointed! This time the animals couldn't fly with us because the Germans said the temperature at the Frankfurt Airport was below freezing. There was no guarantee the animals would be taken inside the building in a timely fashion. Therefore, they couldn't leave Florida. What could we do? School was starting, and we had to get back. We couldn't change our flight from Atlanta because flights to Europe are made in advance. We'd be stuck for days until the weather in Germany warmed to above freezing. We called our friend from Turkey. Would she come and get them and ship them to us later? What else could we do? Meanwhile, Delta Airlines called the officials in Frankfurt. Was there another solution to this problem? After all, we were such good Delta customers that they'd sent us two Waterford brandy snifters years ago.

Frankfurt wanted a letter from a Florida vet who knew the animals to determine if sitting in the cold would traumatize the young pets. Our friend from Turkey really didn't want to mother our two small animals along with hers, so she, being an enterprising former DoDDS teacher, called one of her student's parents who just happened to be a veterinarian. The vet called our vet and the two doctors came up with a feasible written statement for the Germans. It was faxed to Delta just in time for us to board the plane to Atlanta. We were assured there would be no problem getting on the Delta flight to Frankfurt in Atlanta.

By that time, I wanted to never return to Destin, never mind that we owned a condo there. Flying into Valpairiso (VPS) is easy but leaving is never easy!

Back at school, my fifth graders never accepted the idea of "the twins." It was too much for their developing brains. Joking was not for them. The usual response was, "But one's a cat and the other is a dog! It's impossible. They can't be twins just because they're the same age and you got them at almost the same time!" One girl, however, wanted to care for TC for us when we went on trips; she knew we treated our student animal helpers well. They always earned money and often got presents from the places we visited.

During another Christmas vacation, the same girl kept TC again. She and her family had lived on post for two years. The day I took TC over for Christmas break, Mom told me they were moving off post in three days! The kids would be starting German school after the holidays. If I had only known so that I could have found another reliable student in time, I would have not left my Nervous Nelly, commonly known as TC, with that family. They were great because they lived on post; TC couldn't get lost on post. And TC does not like change.

If you think children are individuals, then you need to know that cats and dogs are too. TC is a nervous cat; if someone clears his throat, the cat runs for cover. Our cleaning lady has been working for us for nine years; she's seen TC only three times because he slinks around the house and hides in strange places when she's cleaning. During parties he hides; he runs when the phone rings.

But off we went to the States for Christmas again. We had a great time catching the sales, seeing the new movies, and visiting friends. When we arrived home, I immediately called TC's cat-sitter. Mom answered the phone; they'd been waiting for the call. It seems TC had gotten loose and run away a few days after they'd moved. He'd been living outdoors in the snow that had started before Christmas. The family hadn't seen him. Tuna fish left outside went uneaten, but sometimes other food was gone. Tuna fish was no mystery. He hates tuna fish! I could have accepted almost anything except the fact that he was living outside in the cold; he'd started out as a wild cat, and now he was back outside again.

Frank and I drove over and walked around, calling him feeling totally frustrated. If only I'd known they were moving in time to find another dependable family. Mom wanted me to take his cage and food with us when we drove home. I said no. We'd need the carrier to take him home once we found him. A week later I put up notices in the German neighborhood, offering a hundred Euros for his return. Mom thought she would have to pay the reward, so two days later she trapped him when he came to the house for food. Amazing what can be achieved when money is involved! The student got to keep the cat-sitting money I'd given her before Christmas, but we made other arrangements for the future.

The next day TC went to the vet. He'd been getting the feline leukemia shots because I still thought of him as a wild cat. If he jumped the fence or ran away, I wanted him protected. All he needed after his vacation in the snow was a good bath. The vet told me how to safely give him a bath; the safety guidelines were for me, not the cat! TC let me bathe him without any protest: no claws, no scratches. He was actually purring! I think he was happy to be a clean kitty again. That was the first and last time he actually lived outdoors, even though later he did decide to jump our one-and-half-meter-high fence. Frank found him right away. The second and last time he jumped the fence, I was over it. I left the garage door cracked; no one searched for him. He came in by himself and didn't run away from home anymore. Doesn't that sound just like a kid seeking some attention?

The Berlin Wall had since come down, so we drove back to Berlin to visit the Pergamon Museum and the Egyptian Museum. The Egyptian Museum has a bust of Nefertiti. Located on the former "free" side of the Wall, we walked to that museum. Our other favorite Berlin museum was located on the former Communist side, and this time we were able to drive and park our car right in front of the Pergamon. The museum was built around the temple stolen from Turkey by the Germans. They had dismantled it, shipped it to Berlin, and reconstructed it for their pleasure. What a change from our last visit to Berlin. We collected a couple of pieces of the Wall for souvenirs, visited a wonderful Balkan restaurant, and shopped.

During another summer vacation we visited three countries that had become independent from the USSR: Estonia, Latvia, and Lithuania. Tallinn was the neatest city, with its Northern Lights, garlic and Russian restaurants, and unusual beer. The market sold hand-knit sweaters for very low prices—but cash only, no credit cards. It's probably changed by now. From Tallinn we took the ferry to Helsinki.

It was my first trip back since the Russian trip from Grafenwoehr. The shopping in the weekly market was great, and Visa was accepted there: fur-lined leather gloves, amber jewelry, hand-knit sweaters, leather jackets and purses, furs, and all the fresh fish you could possibly want! Helsinki is very expensive, so go on a tour for the nicest hotels. We had pizza for our only meal there before we flew back to Frankfurt via Estonia Airlines. After a week of Russian and garlic meals, plus some local specialties, pizza was the order of the night; it was Italian, with Italian wine!

We often remember the nights of light in Tallinn. For some reason, there were no rolladens in Estonia which we loved so much in Germany; we had no problem sleeping though as long as the drapes were closed tightly. In Europe rolladens are used to close out the sun if it's too hot or for privacy at night when the lights are on. No one can see in, and they also keep the house warmer during the cold winter months. In downtown Miami the stores in the "bad" part of town used them too; they were called hurricane shutters and kept the stores from being robbed. It was strange to be on the streets at night with lots of natural light. I wouldn't like a steady diet of it, but for one week, we survived!

The other two countries were nice to visit but didn't have the personality of Tallinn. Amber was cheaper than in Tallinn or Moscow and St. Petersburg. The settings were also different, but those we saw were set in real silver. Riga is a navy port and was used during the WWII. The perogies were the snack of choice and good. Not as good as the ones you get in Poland, however!

If we were to go back to revisit the Balkans, we'd probably limit the trip to Tallinn and then take the ferry across the Gulf of Finland to Helsinki. The flights on Estonia Air are cheap, and the comfort is no worse than other airlines we've flown in around the world.

❧ CHAPTER 34 ❧
2005–2007
Kaiserslautern
India

THREE YEARS LATER WE MOVED TO KAISERSLAUTERN; FRANK DROVE TO BAUMHOLDER each school day, and I taught a 4/5 combination class at Kaiserslautern Elementary. We booked a tour to India over Thanksgiving week. When we arrived at the Frankfurt Airport to check in for our flight, we discovered the local American travel agency had not gotten our visas. The Indian visa office in Frankfurt was to blame, they said. We've dealt with the Indian visa office, and it takes two visits and lots of money for a tourist visa. We couldn't go to India as planned, so we worked instead. Not a pleasant substitution for a week in warm India.

Two years later we got our own visas and toured India on two separate trips: once during spring break and the second time in early July. Seeing the Taj Mahal was breathtaking, but Jaipur, the pink city, and Jodphur, the blue city, were also worth the money. In Jodphur we followed in the steps of Richard Gere; everywhere we shopped, he'd been there first! His autographed picture hung on quite a few walls. In one particular textile warehouse, Mr. Gere bought one hundred silk scarves for one hundred good friends; we bought a measly four! I guess that meant either we only had four good friends or we were not rich. Go figure.

In July we went to Udaipur and followed in the footsteps of Mrs. Clinton and Chelsea. They'd stayed on the island in the castle, which cost $2,000 per night. We stayed in a four-star hotel on the mainland, which matched our standard of traveling and were very content. But Uncle Sam wasn't paying for our trip.

We seemed to follow the Clintons around too. They bought a huge vase, pronounced "vaze," as all expensive vases should be, which was almost as tall as I am. We didn't buy anything from that particular merchant.

The jewelry store got our money. According to the German jeweler who appraised our purchases, we got very good deals! The Clintons had not visited our jeweler; I'm not sure what that means. Bill was not with them, so maybe he was the buyer of expensive trinkets! The jeweler had been suggested by our tour guide, and we recommend the store to all our friends. The tour guides only take you to reputable merchants.

The only time we had a problem with our purchases in India was when we found nothing we liked in a recommended store; the local female guide suggested the store across the street. We ended up returning the jewelry three months later. Once I'd had the purchases appraised by our German jeweler, I wrote to the tour agency in Garmisch and complained. We went back to that particular store accompanied by the agency's vice president. Evidently the tour agency had contacted the jeweler in the months before we returned and explained we wanted all of our money back in return for the jewelry. We were lucky in that we could actually hop on a plane and return as cheaply as we did. You would spend a lot more money trying to do that from the States. Unfortunately, this particular merchant traveled to Las Vegas all the time to do jewelry shows. I shudder to think what kind of overpriced jewelry Americans are buying from him and I doubt disgruntled customers often return merchandise. But we had a year-long visa, and we used it! We also got to see more of that beautiful country.

Driving through Delhi was a trip. The cows rule the streets, and all traffic watches out for them. We stayed in an old British hotel that had stars, great rooms, and excellent food, including homemade mango ice cream. We returned to that hotel on our second trip, but mangoes were out of season, I guess, and we will probably return again if we're ever back in Delhi.

A friend in Taegu had visited India with a group of teachers many years before we made it there. After his stories, I was always scared to death at the thought of traveling there. One teacher ate something that disagreed with her and actually died. Another tale happened at a religious site. Under the table were baskets filled with snakes; the other teachers didn't know it, but my friend did! I *had* to stay in nice places because of his stories.

While we were in Tampa, the newspaper ran a story about a girl who'd gone to an Indian hospital with appendicitis; her appendix was removed, and she flew home when she was released from the hospital. After returning to the States, she still did not feel very well, so she went to her physician. While she was under, not only had her appendix been removed but also one of her kidneys! Stories like that kept me from traveling to India for many years.

We loved both our visits. One day I plan to go through all the aggravation with the Indian Consulate in Frankfurt again so that we can visit Mumbai and Goa and maybe spend some time on one of their white, sandy beaches. The pictures look spectacular; I can only imagine how beautiful they would be in person.

Back in Germany, we decided TC needed another cat to play with. Big mistake! On our next trip home we visited the Cattery and got Yoda. He was so small he fit into my hand with lots of room left over. We dreaded taking him back through VPS, but that time, believe it or not, we had absolutely no problem. When we carried him through passport control, the checker thought he was just so-o-o cute. He traveled under our seat the entire trip. When we got him home, TC took one look at him and snarled. He's never quit snarling! Yoda has grown up to be best pals with our latest schnauzer, and they both sleep together. TC does not sleep with either of them. Yoda is now affectionately called our Fat Cat. Why we ever thought he might die from malnutrition, I can't imagine!

❧ CHAPTER 35 ❧

2007–2010
Vogelweh Elementary School
Sharm El Shek

I MOVED ACROSS THE STREET FROM KAISERSLAUTERN ELEMENTARY (KES) TO Vogelweh Elementary (VES). Suddenly, I experienced allergies and lung problems. The buildings were infested with mold. After visiting the local ear, nose, and throat (ENT) specialist many, many times over a three-year period, he got me a transfer out of those disease-causing buildings back to Ramstein. If I had continued to teach there, I would have ended up with a permanent case of asthma. Vogelweh had been converted from one of Hitler's army-headquarters building into an elementary school. When teachers complained about the mold, the school officials had that particular room repainted.

Our last visit to Egypt was to a beach resort at Sharm El Shek. It renewed my previous impressions of the country. I didn't want to ever live there or teach at the University of Cairo; if I could help it, I'd never go back again. It was smelly, hotter than ever, dry, and the men hadn't changed at all. The men bugged the women tourists to death. I'd never travel to Egypt by myself! Tours are fine if your tour includes thirty people. The other option would be to go with a man and hang onto his arm the whole time as if he owned you.

We ate great lobster for the first time in Egypt. It was the most expensive lobster we've ever ordered, especially from a city on the water. One night we had lobster from the Red Sea and the next night lobster from the Mediterranean. The Red Sea was my favorite; it was thick and chewy. The Mediterranean version tasted like normal lobster from Maine or the Gulf.

Our week was finally up, and I was a happy camper. It was much too hot for me, and I couldn't walk around and people-watch as much as I love to do. Then a natural disaster affected both the US and Europe. The volcano in Iceland blew its top. All flights were canceled due to the dust in the air. Teachers were stranded in America and all over Europe. The schools back home continued using subs. We had to stay where we were. I wrote my travel agent in Kaiserslautern and begged her to get us out of our hot environment and back to cool, wonderful Germany! When the airways began to reopen, a plane was sent to Sharm El Shek to pick up some special travelers who were flying with a certain tour company. She told us we might be able to get a seat, but there was no guarantee. We'd have to talk ourselves onto the flight! That's what we did. We grabbed our suitcases, checked out of our nice hotel, and told them we might be back.

Frank handled the luggage, and I talked our way onto an Air Berlin charter flight headed for Dusseldorf; there was another charter flying to Nuremberg, but we opted for the flight closer to Frankfurt. While we were waiting for our flight to board, we visited the small gift shop. I got the chance to round out my collection of orange stones. Not only did they have a ring adorned with a massive orange stone but enough loose stones to make a bracelet. The salesman told me the stones were only found in Egypt; he described them as amethysts that had been laser-heated until the color changed to orange. Who knows if that's true? I repeated this story to a jeweler in Athens, whose store I've visited for years. He wants me to bring one of the pieces on our next trip. It might be a true story. Maybe Sharm El Shek wasn't so bad after all!

We landed in cold Dusseldorf wearing our hot-weather clothing and caught a train to the Frankfurt airport to pick up our car. We were happy and felt very lucky to have gotten a free ride on another airline, not our own. It seems all the European airlines were working together to solve the European tourist dilemma. We missed two days of school; others missed the entire week. One couple was stranded in Tenerife for an extra week at no expense to themselves. Now, that's the place to get stranded!

❧ CHAPTER 36 ❧
2010–2013
Ramstein Intermediate School

AFTER THREE UNPLEASANT YEARS AND NOT BECAUSE OF THE STUDENTS, TEACHERS, or parents at VES, I transferred back to Ramstein Intermediate School. The elementary school had been turned into two separate schools due to the large population. By that time the military was downsizing—bases were closing, teachers were retiring—but Ramstein continued to grow.

Our best trip was to Poland and Prague after school let out that first summer. We drove to the Polish pottery area, which bypassed Dresden and the Hard Rock Cafe. After we shopped till we dropped buying Polish pottery, we headed to Prague. The pottery at the factories was cheaper than the Officers Wives Club (OWC) bazaars and the selection greater. Unfortunately, Poland was not in our GPS. We had to wander through the back roads until we hit the Czech Republic; from then on we sailed right to our hotel using GPS. Prague is now a modern city. Plus it was June, and that meant warmth! The Hard Rock Cafe was alive and well there, just as in Krakow, Poland.

During one long weekend break we flew to Krakow on Lot Airlines and spent three sunny days in May, enjoying the city's sights and markets. One day included a tour of Auschwitz. Like Dachau, we had to visit it once, and once was more than enough. The people were friendly and shopping was plentiful. Flying on Lot was just as cheap and comfortable as Estonia Air Lines.

The following year we headed to Florence to see David again. He was still there in all his splendor, right where we'd left him the last time, basking in the Florence sun. Gold and leather are still good buys, but I was into summer dresses. Italians make the brightest sundresses, with Spain a close second. Greece is third.

After three years as Ramstein's math coach, I decided to retire.

❧ CHAPTER 37 ❧

June 30, 2013
Retirement

My goal after retiring was to "do nothing" constructive, which to me meant no part time job or volunteer work. Retirement meant a trip each month for one year. In September, I rode the train to Paris and took a French cooking class featuring *Sauces.* In October, I flew to Kusadasi, Turkey, for a week, but I spent lots of time in Izmir. November we flew to Djerba, Tunesia, during Thanksgiving week for our annual week of sun. Then it was ten weeks in Tenerife, and then I headed back to Paris for a two-day *Bread Making* class. April meant a trip to Ireland: we enjoyed a driving tour around the island, with a side trip to Belfast. I'm considering Tenerife again in May but just for a couple of weeks. August brings another trip to Paris for two classes *Macaroons* and *Hors d'oeuvres in a Glass,* September brings *Terrines* (my favorite) and my last French-cooking classes in December are *Desserts in a Glass* and *Foi Gras.* A friend told me about an Italian cooking school located on Lake Garda, and I'm investigating their schedules.

My dream is to open a small restaurant with about ten tables; the menu would be very simple. Prices would be set. There would be no substitutions! The menu would include three starters, three entrees, and three desserts from which to choose. The restaurant would be open for business six days per week with different themes: Tuesday Mexican; Wednesday Italian; Thursday Tex Mex; Friday American; Saturday French; Sunday brunch only. Reservations would be required, of course. My husband doesn't like fish, and I'm allergic to shellfish, so seafood would never be a choice. We'd offer vegetarian choices since my middle name is Vegetable-Lover. Prices would be moderate to expensive, depending on the entrees and wine choices made. Liqueurs and dessert coffees would be available.

Back when I lived in Graf, some of my friends flew to Tenerife for spring break. They came back sorry they'd gone! It had rained every day for seven days which spoiled their beach time; they'd suffered through by playing cards all day. That story settled it for me. I never wanted to waste my time and money on the Canary Islands.

Many years and many countries later, some good friends from KES went to Tenerife for Christmas week. They came back reeling in the glory of seven days in heaven on Earth. We'd been to the beaches of Tunisia, Hawaii, Egypt, and Israel, just to name a few. Why not try the Canary Islands next? Surely it wouldn't rain for seven days if we went?

The next Christmas we took the plunge and went for one glorious week. The following Christmas we went for two glorious weeks—and the next Christmas and the next. Somewhere along the way, we went for spring break, then for a week in August, and finally a week in June. We never got rained out. There was a sprinkle one Christmas, and maybe two sprinkles on another visit, but we had found the Hawaiian Islands of the European Atlantic. If we could have bought a house, apartment, or condo on the islands, we would have.

In April of my last year of teaching, I wrote my travel agent, who continued to walk on water, and asked her to get me an apartment in Southern Tenerife for three months. She could only cover us for ten weeks, but that was enough for me to try writing about the fun times in DoDDS. I left December 4 as the bad winter weather in Germany was just getting underway.

As I'm writing this, I'm enjoying the Tenerife sun and 70 F. weather. It's been a very relaxing time, and I've accomplished more than I ever could have at home with all the interruptions by Sweetie Pie, our latest miniature schnauzer, chasing Yoda, the fat cat, or TC, the terrible cat or tabby cat or tomcat, depending on his moods and mine, around the downstairs. I eat out every day, but only once per day. I've walked an average of five miles every day for the past fifty-eight days and my clothes keep getting tighter!

I had just twelve days left before I fly back to dreary Germany. I took the day off from writing in order to give my fingers a rest. As I was out walking, I noticed a new-style dress hanging from one of the nails on the outside of a beach store. I went in to check it out. As I was deciding which color combination I liked the best, I was also checking out the sizes. There were small, medium-large, large-X large, and XX large dresses hanging. I looked at the M-L and tried to imagine it fitting me. Then I looked at the L-XL. For some reason, they both looked like the same dimensions! Hmm. One was black, red, and gray, and the other was navy, gray, and black. Next I held up a turquoise-and-gray combination, but it looked too small. Maybe it would fit. Something just didn't look right about the three dresses. I measured the smallest next to the XXL one, and they were both the same! That could not possibly be the case, so I measured two other ones. They were the same too. What a mystery!

I finally had to ask the guy who was hovering around, waiting for me to make a decision. Did this tourist lady want the 10 Euro small, the 10 Euro M-L, or was she going to settle on the 10 Euro L-XXL? I showed him how I had compared the two dresses and mentioned they were the same. His comment was any of the dresses would fit me. Decide which color I liked, or, better yet, buy two! No, no, no, I argued. I wanted it to fit me, not be too big. He finally understood my problem, thank goodness. The labels didn't matter. All the dresses were one size, he tried to explain. The labels were just sewed on to please tourist ladies like myself who wanted a smaller, not larger, sized label! I ended up buying two.

As I walked away with my new smaller-labeled purchases, I remembered all the other dresses I'd bypassed in the last eight weeks because the labels had said L or XL or even yet XXL! I had denied myself some great deals! What a tourist trap! It had taken me six visits to the island in six years to finally learn their sales gimmick!

That also explained the dress I'd looked at the week before; the style, material, and price had been fine, but it had been grossly too big. The salesgirl had smiled and told me to wait a minute as she rummaged around under the counter. She came up with a dress still in cellophane that met my criteria. She happily told me the one in my hand had been stretched out of shape by women trying it on. Now her story made a lot more sense to me!

I've enjoyed French food in nearby Las Gilletas and Tex Mex down the street. I skipped both Burger King and Micky D's, helped the Hard Rock Cafe open their newest restaurant, and found the restaurant of my dreams. Its name is simply Mexican Restaurant, but it reeks of Mexico. We hadn't had Mexican food that good since we traveled to Mexico one Christmas break from Tampa. I planned to take a menu home with me to remind me of the dishes. I'm sure I can figure out the recipes once I'm back in my gourmet kitchen at home.

According to the English newspaper, the Spanish love to spend Christmas in Tenerife; the Russians number 33 percent of the visitors in recent years, and there's more British English heard here than any other language. American visitors are few and far between according to the locals, who love to hear American English being spoken.

If you're on a budget, come on an all-inclusive tour. If you want to stay longer and more cheaply, rent an apartment. You'll find more than three hundred restaurants outside your door to try and all the water sports your heart could ever desire.

Along with that temperatures are cool in the early morning, warming to between 70 and 90 F during the day depending on the season, and cool air flows again about five in the afternoon. The sunsets are magnificent. The Canarians love tourists, and I sincerely believe you won't experience seven days of rain. I'm now thoroughly convinced my friends from Grafenwoehr exaggerated!

By the way, Canarians don't claim to be Spanish; they'd love to get their independence from Spain, but according to my historian husband, it will never happen! Why? They've discovered oil on one of the islands!

I left Tenerife on February 9 with 85 percent of this manuscript finished. I could never get myself into the mood to finish it back in Germany, so I told my husband good-bye for another two weeks. Three days are left of my second week, and I'm finished, except for the final editing.

I was going to include *all* my delicious recipes from my time overseas, but I've decided to write another book and make it a cookbook. Therefore, I only included a few of my really good recipes. After the cookbook is finished, I want to finish two or three children's books. All I need is an illustrator who can draw animals in action.

If you're thinking of teaching as a career and you like change, teaching for the military is a lot of fun. If you're stubborn or too set in your ways, stay at home where life is more "normal."

If you enjoyed these stories, just remember that I only told you the fun stuff. There's a lot more to tell, but I'll never be able to tell the whole truth! Every educational system has ugly stories, and DoDDS is not immune either. If you're a military parent, then DoDDS is most likely the best system you'll ever encounter for your children. DoDDS teachers may get paid more than stateside teachers, but they more than earn every penny. Remember, nothing is free with Uncle Sam! There are lots of disadvantages to living outside the good ole US of A.

Enjoy more recipes in 2016 with my newest endeavor: a cookbook, describing ALL my recipes, entitled "My Love Affair with Cooking."

Best-Ever Chocolate Cake

Ingredients

    4 ounces unsweetened chocolate
    ½ cup vegetable oil
    ½ cup butter, room temperature
    2 cups sugar
    3 eggs, beaten
    1 teaspoon vanilla
    2 cups all-purpose flour
    1/3 cup cocoa
    1 teaspoon salt
    2 teaspoons baking soda
    2 teaspoons baking powder
    1/3 cup buttermilk
    3 cups grated zucchini
    ½ cup chopped walnuts

Thin chocolate bars for between bottom and middle layer. You need enough to cover the layer.

Directions

Melt chocolate and oil in a small saucepan over very low heat.
Cream butter; add sugar, eggs, and vanilla; beat well. Add melted chocolate and mix. Sift flour, cocoa, salt, baking soda, and baking powder and stir into the batter; add buttermilk. Blend zucchini and nuts into the batter.

Spray 2 (9-inch) cake pans with Baker's Joy. Divide the batter between the pans. Bake for 40 minutes at 350 F. Cool completely before frosting.

Frosting

    1 (6-ounce) package semisweet chocolate chips
    ½ cup light cream
    1 cup butter
    2-1/2 cups powdered sugar

Directions

In medium saucepan, combine chocolate chips, cream, butter; stir over medium heat until smooth. Remove from heat. With whisk, blend in 2 1/2 cups powdered sugar. In a bowl set over ice, beat until it holds shape.

*Find the thinnest chocolate bars (In my German grocery store they are about 2 x 3" and it takes about 10-12 to cover the area. Some overlap. The chocolate bars need to be paper thin or cutting the cake takes muscles.) you can and place them between the layers.

*I copied this idea from a well-known restaurant chain in Barcelona; our dessert that night was superb. It was the best chocolate cake I've ever had in a restaurant. Usually, the homemade cakes are better.

Refrigerate cake at least 1 hour before serving. Freezes well.

Gran Marnier Cranberry Sauce

Ingredients
    1 bag (24 ounces) fresh cranberries.
    1 cup sugar
    grated rind from one orange
    ½ cup Gran Marnier

Note: You can substitute Triple Sec or Cointreau but do a taste test to see if you need to add more sugar. Original Gran Marnier is sweeter than substitutes.

Directions
Wash and pick out the bad berries; let them dry or use paper towels to dry them more quickly.

Combine all ingredients in a lasagna pan. Set aside 20 to 30 minutes or overnight, covered, to let the berries marinate in the liquor.

Preheat oven to 325 F.

Cover the dish with foil and bake for 40 minutes.

If they aren't bubbling and smelling absolutely out of this world, stir and bake about 10 minutes longer.

For a larger crowd: use 3 bags of cranberries and 1 cup sugar, the rind from 2 large oranges, and 1 ½ cups Gran Marnier. This will take longer to cook so keep an eye on your oven. When it smells heavenly, then it's probably ready.

INDEX OF RECIPES

DRINKS

MAIN DISHES

MARINADES

MUSLI